THE READING OF COMPLETE ENGLISH CLASSICS

IN THE COMMON SCHOOL

SPECIAL METHOD

IN THE

READING OF COMPLETE ENGLISH CLASSICS

CHAPTER I

EDUCATIONAL VALUE OF LITERATURE

The gradual introduction of the choicer products of literature into the grades of the common school has been going on for several years. Bringing the school children face to face with the thoughts of the masters has had often a thrilling effect, and the feeling has spread among teachers that a new door has been opened into what Ruskin calls "The King's Gardens." As we stand at this open portal to the Elysian Fields of literature, there may fall upon us something of the beauty, something even of the solemn stillness, of the arched cathedral with its golden windows. But how inadequate is the Gothic cathedral, or the Greek temple, to symbolize the temple of literature.

Within less than a score of years there has been such reading of varied literary masterpieces by children as to bring us face to face with a problem of prime significance in education, the place and importance of literature in the education of American children.

Millions of children are introduced yearly to bookland, and it is a matter of greater importance than what Congress does, what provision is made for these oncoming millions in the sunlit fields and forest glades of literature, where the boys and girls walk in happy companionship with the "wisest and wittiest" of our race. We have now had enough experience with these treasures of culture to get a real foretaste of the feast prepared for the growing youth. We know that their appetites are keen and their digestive powers strong. It is incumbent upon educators to get a comprehensive survey of this land and to estimate its resources. Other fields of study, like natural science, geography, music, etc., are undergoing the same scrutiny as to their educative value. Literature, certainly a peer in the hierarchy of great studies, if not supreme in value above others, is one of the most difficult to estimate. Tangible proofs of the vital culture-force of good literature upon growing minds can be given in many individual cases. But to what degree it has general or universal fitness to awaken, strengthen, and refine all minds, is in dispute.

It seems clear, at least, that only those who show taste and enthusiasm for a choice piece of literature can teach it with success. This requirement of appreciation and enjoyment of the study is more imperative in literature, because its appeal is not merely to the intellect and the reason, as in other studies, but especially to the emotions and higher æsthetic judgments, to moral and religious sentiment in ideal representation.

It has been often observed that discussions of the superior educative value of literature before bodies of teachers, while entertaining and delightful, fall far short of lasting results because of the teachers' narrow experience with literature. In the case of many teachers, the primitive alphabet of literary appreciation is lacking, and the most enthusiastic appeals to the charm and exaltation of such studies fall harmless. Yet literature in the schools is hopeless without teachers who have felt at home in this delightsome land, this most real world of ideal strength and beauty.

The discussion of the subject for teachers is beset, therefore, with peculiar and seemingly insurmountable difficulties. The strength, charm, and refinement of literature are known only to those who have read the masters with delight, while even people of cultured taste listen doubtfully to the praise of authors they have never read. To one enamoured of the music of Tennyson's songs, the very suggestion of "In Memoriam" awakens enthusiasm. To one who has not read Tennyson and his like, silence on the subject is golden. To those not much travelled in the fields of literature, there is danger of speaking in an unknown tongue, while they, of all others, need a plain and convincing word. To speak this plain and convincing word to those who may have acquired but little relish for literature, and that little only in the fragmentary selections of the school readers, is a high and difficult aim. But teachers are willing to learn, and to discover new sources of enthusiasm in their profession. It is probable, also, that the original capacity to enjoy great literature is much more common than is often supposed, and that the great average of teachers is quite capable of receiving this powerful stimulus. The fact is, our common schools have done so little, till of late, to cultivate this fine taste, that we have faint reason to expect it in our teachers.

Overwhelmed as we are with the folly of indulging in the praise of literature before many whose ears have been but poorly attuned to the sweet melody or majestic rhythm of the masters, we still make bold to grapple with this argument. There is surely no subject to which the teachers need more to open their eyes and ears and better nature, so as to take in the enrichment it affords. There is encouragement in the fact that many teachers fully appreciate the worth of these writers, and have succeeded in making their works beautiful and educative to the children. Very many other teachers are capable of the full refreshing enjoyment of classic works, when their attention and labor are properly expended upon them. The colleges, universities, high schools, and normal schools have largely abandoned the dull epitomizing of literature, the talk about authors, for the study of the works themselves of the masters. The consequence is, that the study of literature in English is becoming an enthusiasm, and teachers of this type are multiplying.

The deeper causes for this widespread lack of literary appreciation among the people, and even among teachers and scholars, is found partly in the practical, scientific, and utilitarian spirit of the age, and partly in the corresponding unliterary courses of study which have prevailed everywhere in our common schools. The absence of literary standards and taste among teachers is due largely to the failure of the schools themselves, hitherto, to cultivate this sort of proficiency. Those very qualities which give to literature its supreme excellence, its poetic beauty, its artistic finish and idealism, are among the highest fruits of culture, and are far more difficult of attainment than mere knowledge. It is no small thing to introduce the rarest and finest culture of the world into the common school, and thus propagate, in the broadest democratic fashion, that which is the peculiar, superior refinement of the choicest spirits of the world. If progress in this direction is slow, we may remember that the best ideals are slow of attainment.

There is also an intangible quality in all first-class literature, which is not capable of exact description or demonstration. George Willis Cooke, in "Poets and Problems" (pp. 31-32), says:—

"Poetry enters into those higher regions of human experience concerning which no definite account can be given; where all words fail; about which all we know is to be obtained by hints, symbols, poetic figures, and imagings. Poetry is truer and more helpful than prose, because it penetrates those regions of feeling, beauty, and spiritual reality, where definitions have no place or justification. There would be no poetry if life were limited to what we can understand; nor would there be any religion. Indeed, the joy, the beauty, and the promise of life would all be gone if there were nothing which reaches beyond our powers of definition. The mystery of existence makes the grandeur and worth of man's nature, as it makes for him his poetry and his religion. Poetry suggests, hints, images forth, what is too wonderful, too transcendent, too near primal reality, too full of life, beauty, and joy, for explanation or comprehension. It embodies man's longing after the Eternal One, expresses his sense of the deep mystery of Being, voices his soul sorrow, illumines his path with hope and objects of beauty. Man's aspiration, his sense of imperfection, his yearning for a sustaining truth and reality, as the life within and over all things, find expression in poetry; because it offers the fittest medium of interpretation for these higher movements of soul. Whenever the soul feels deeply, or is stirred by a great thought, the poetic form of utterance at once becomes the most natural and desirable for its loving and faithful interpretation."

This intangible excellence of superior literature, which defies all exact measurement by the yardstick, puzzles the practical man and the scientist. There is no way of getting at it with their tools and measurements. They are very apt to give it up in disgust and dismiss it with some uncomplimentary name. But Shakespeare's mild reign continues, and old Homer sings his deathless song to those who wish to hear.

Teachers need both the exact methods of science and the spiritual life of the poets, and we may well spend some pains in finding out the life-giving properties of good literature.

Lowell, in his "Books and Libraries," says:—

"To wash down the drier morsels that every library must necessarily offer at its board, let there be plenty of imaginative literature, and let its range be not too narrow to stretch from Dante to the elder Dumas. The world of the imagination is not the world of abstraction and nonentity, as some conceive, but a world formed out of chaos by a sense of the beauty that is in man and the earth on which he dwells. It is the realm of Might-be, our haven of refuge from the shortcomings and disillusions of life. It is, to quote Spenser, who knew it well,—

"'The world's sweet inn from care and wearisome turmoil.' Do we believe, then, that God gave us in mockery this splendid faculty of sympathy with things that are a joy forever? For my part, I believe that the love and study of works of imagination is of practical utility in a country so profoundly material (or, as we like to call it, practical) in its leading tendencies as ours. The hunger after purely intellectual delights, the content with ideal possessions, cannot but be good for us in maintaining a wholesome balance of the character and of the faculties. I for one shall never be persuaded that Shakespeare left a less useful legacy to his countrymen than Watt. We hold all the deepest, all the highest, satisfactions of life as tenants of imagination. Nature will keep up the supply of what are called hard-headed people without our help, and, if it come to that, there are other as good uses for heads as at the end of battering-rams."

"But have you ever rightly considered what the mere ability to read means? That it is the key which admits us to the whole world of thought and fancy and imagination? to the company of saint and sage, of the wisest and wittiest at their wisest and wittiest moments? That it enables us to see with the keenest eyes, hear with the finest ears, and listen to the sweetest voices of all time? More than that, it annihilates time and space for us; it revives for us without a miracle the Age of Wonder, endowing us with the shoes of swiftness and the cap of darkness, so that we walk invisible like fern-seed, and witness unharmed the plague at Athens or Florence or London; accompany Cæsar on his marches, or look in on Catiline in council with his fellow-conspirators, or Guy Fawkes in the cellar of St. Stephen's. We often hear of people who will descend to any servility, submit to any insult, for the sake of getting themselves or their children into what is euphemistically called good society. Did it ever occur to them that there is a select society of all the centuries to which they and theirs can be admitted for the asking, a society, too, which will not involve them in ruinous expense, and still more ruinous waste of time and health and faculties?

"The riches of scholarship, the benignities of literature, defy fortune and outlive calamity. They are beyond the reach of thief or moth or rust. As they cannot be inherited, so they cannot be alienated. But they may be shared, they may be distributed."

This notion of the select companionship of books finds also happy expression in Ruskin's "Sesame and Lilies":—

"We may intrude ten minutes' talk on a cabinet minister, answered probably with words worse than silence, being deceptive; or snatch, once or twice in our lives, the privilege of throwing a bouquet in the path of a princess, or arresting the kind glance of a queen. And yet these momentary chances we covet; and spend our years, and passions, and powers in pursuit of little more than these; while, meantime, there is a society continually open to us, of people who will talk to us as long as we like, whatever our rank or occupation;—talk to us in the best words they can choose, and with thanks if we listen to them. And this society, because it is so numerous and so gentle,—and can be kept waiting round us all day long, not to grant audience, but to gain it; kings and statesmen lingering patiently in those plainly furnished and narrow anterooms, our bookcase shelves,—we make no account of that company,—perhaps never listen to a word they would say, all day long!

"This court of the past differs from all living aristocracy in this: it is open to labor and to merit, but to nothing else. No wealth will bribe, no name overawe, no artifice deceive, the guardian of those Elysian gates. In the deep sense, no vile or vulgar person ever enters there. At the portières of that silent Faubourg St.-Germain, there is but brief question, 'Do you deserve to enter?' 'Pass. Do you ask to be the companions of nobles? Make yourself noble, and you shall be. Do you long for the conversation of the wise? Learn to understand it, and you shall hear it. But on other terms?— no. If you will not rise to us, we cannot stoop to you. The living lord may assume courtesy, the living philosopher explain his thought to you with considerable pain; but here we neither feign nor interpret; you must rise to the level of our thoughts if you would be gladdened by them, and share our feelings, if you would recognize our presence.'"

Wordsworth says:—

"Books, we know,
Are a substantial world, both pure and good;

Round these, with tendrils strong as flesh and blood,
Our pastime and our happiness will grow."

Carlyle says:—

"We learn to read, in various languages, in various sciences; we learn the alphabet and letters of all manner of Books. But the place where we are to get knowledge, even theoretic knowledge, is the Books themselves! It depends on what we read, after all manner of Professors have done their best for us. The true University of these days is a Collection of Books."

Were we willing to accept the testimony of great writers and thinkers, we should but too quickly acknowledge the supreme value of books. James Baldwin, in the first chapter of his "Book Lover," has collected more than a score of like utterances of great writers "In Praise of Books." Such testimony may at least suggest to some of us who have drunk but sparingly of the refreshing springs of literature, that there are better things in store for us.

We will first inquire into those vital elements of strength which are peculiar to literature.

One of the elements that goes into the make-up of a masterpiece of literature is its underlying, permanent truth. Whether written to-day or in earlier centuries, it must contain lasting qualities that do not fade away or bleach out or decay. Time and weather do not stain or destroy its merit. Some classics, as Gray's "Elegy," or "Thanatopsis," are like cut diamonds. The quality that gives them force and brilliancy is inherent, and the form in which they appear has been wrought out by an artist. The fundamental value of a classic is the deep, significant truth which, like the grain in fine woods, is wrought into its very structure. The artist who moulds a masterpiece like "Enoch Arden" or "The Scarlet Letter" is not a writer of temporary fame. The truth to which he feels impelled to give expression is strong, natural, human truth, which has no beginning and no end. It is true forever. Schiller's William Tell, though idealized, is a human hero with the hearty thoughts of a real man. Shylock is a Jew of flesh and blood, who will laugh if he is tickled, and break into anger if he is thwarted. The true poet builds upon eternal foundations. The bookmaker or rhymer is satisfied with empty or fleeting thoughts and with a passing notoriety. New books are often caught up and blazoned as classics which a few years reveal as patchwork and tinsel. Time is a sure test. Showy tinsel rusts and dulls its lustre, while simple poetic truth shines with growing brightness.

Schlegel, in his "Dramatic Art and Literature," thus contrasts the false and the true (pp. 18-19):—

"Poetry, taken in its widest acceptation, as the power of creating what is beautiful, and representing it to the eye or the ear, is a universal gift of Heaven, being shared to a certain extent even by those whom we call barbarians and savages. Internal excellence is alone decisive, and where this exists we must not allow ourselves to be repelled by the external appearance. Everything must be traced up to the root of human nature: if it has sprung from thence, it has an undoubted worth of its own; but if, without possessing a living germ, it is merely externally attached thereto, it will never thrive nor acquire a proper growth. Many productions which appear at first sight dazzling phenomena in the province of the fine arts, and which as a whole have been honored with the appellation of works of a golden age, resemble the mimic gardens of children: impatient to witness the work of their hands, they break off here and there branches and flowers, and plant them in the earth; everything at first assumes a noble appearance: the childish gardener struts proudly up and down among his showy beds, till the rootless plants begin to droop, and hang their withered leaves and blossoms, and nothing soon remains but the bare twigs, while the dark forest, on which no art or care was ever bestowed, and which towered up toward heaven long before human remembrance, bears every blast unshaken, and fills the solitary beholder with religious awe."

In his "Poets and Problems," George Willis Cooke fitly portrays the poet's function (pp. 42, 32, and 44):—

"The poet must be either a teacher or an artist; or, what is better, he may be both in one. Therefore, he can never stop at form or at what delights and charms merely. He must go on to the expression of something of deep and real abidingness of thought and beauty. This comes at last to be the real thing for which he works, which he seeks to bring into expression with such power and grandeur in it as he can produce, and which he wills to send forth for the sake of this higher impression on the world."

"Man has within him a need for the food which does not perish; he always is finding anew that he cannot live by bread alone. His mind will crave truth, his heart love, somewhat to satisfy the inward needs of life. A heavenly homesickness will draw him away from the material to those æsthetic and spiritual realities which are at the source of the truest poetry. Whenever these wants find fit interpretation, the poet and the poetic method of expression appear and give to them outward forms of beauty. Consequently the poet is

> 'One in whom persuasion and belief
> Have ripened into faith, and faith become
> A passionate intuition.'

"The true poet is the man of his time who is most alive, who feels, sees, and knows the most. In the measure of his life he is the greatest man of his age and country. His eye sees farther and more clearly; his heart beats more warmly and with a more universal sympathy; his thought runs deeper and with a swifter current, than is the case with other men. He is the oracle and guide, the inspirer and the friend, of those to whom he sings. He creates life under the ribs of dead tradition; he illumines the present with heart flames of beaconing truth, and he makes the future seem like home joys far off, but drawing ever nigher. The poet is the world's lover."

Emerson found the Greeks standing as close to nature and truth as himself ("Essay on History"):—

"The costly charm of the ancient tragedy, and indeed of all old literature, is, that the persons speak simply,—speak as persons who have great good sense without knowing it, before yet the reflective habit has become the predominant habit of the mind. Our admiration of the antique is not admiration of the old, but of the natural. The Greeks are not reflective, but perfect in their senses and in their health, with the finest physical organization in the world. Adults acted with the simplicity and grace of children."

In his "Defence of Poetry" Shelley says:—

"Poetry thus makes immortal all that is best and most beautiful in the world; it arrests the vanishing apparitions which haunt the interlunations of life, and, veiling them or in language or in form, sends them forth among mankind, bearing sweet news of kindred joy to those with whom their sisters abide—abide, because there is no portal of expression from the caverns of the spirit which they inhabit into the universe of things. Poetry redeems from decay the visitations of the divinity in man."

Carlyle, in his "Heroes and Hero-worship," portrays the deeper art and insight of the poet thus:—

"For my own part, I find considerable meaning in the old vulgar distinction of Poetry being metrical, having music in it, being a Song. Truly, if pressed to give a definition, one might say this as soon as anything else: If your delineation be authentically musical, musical not in word only, but in heart and substance, in all the thoughts and utterances of it, in the whole conception of it, then it will be poetical; if not, not. Musical: how much lies in that! A musical thought is one spoken by a mind that has penetrated into the inmost heart of the thing; detected the inmost mystery of it, namely the melody that lies hidden in it; the inward harmony of coherence which is its soul, whereby it exists, and has a right to be, here in this world. All inmost things, we may say, are melodious; naturally utter themselves in Song. The meaning of Song goes deep. Who is there that, in logical words, can express the effect music has upon us? A kind of inarticulate unfathomable speech, which leads us to the edge of the Infinite, and lets us for moments gaze into that!

"Nay all speech, even the commonest speech, has something of song in it: not a parish in the world but has its parish-accent;—the rhythm or tune to which the people there sing what they have to say! Accent is a kind of chanting; all men have accent of their own,—though they only notice that of others. Observe, too, how all passionate language does of itself become musical,—with a finer music than the mere accent; the speech of a man even in zealous anger becomes a chant, a song. All deep things are Song. It seems somehow the very central essence of us, Song; as if all the rest were but wrappages and hulls. The primal element of us; of us, and of all things. The Greeks fabled of Sphere-Harmonies: it was the feeling they had of the inner structure of Nature; that the soul of all her voices and utterances was perfect music. Poetry, therefore, we will call musical Thought. The Poet is he who thinks in that manner. At bottom, it turns still on power of intellect;

it is a man's sincerity and depth of vision that makes him a Poet. See deep enough, and you see musically; the heart of Nature being everywhere music, if you can only reach it."

"Or indeed we may say again, it is in what I called Portrait-painting, delineating of men and things, especially of men, that Shakespeare is great. All the greatness of the man comes out decisively here. It is unexampled, I think, that calm creative perspicacity of Shakespeare. The thing he looks at reveals not this or that face of it, but its inmost heart, and generic secret: it dissolves itself as in light before him, so that he discerns the perfect structure of it. Creative, we said: poetic creation, what is this, too, but seeing the thing sufficiently? The word that will describe the thing, follows of itself from such clear intense sight of the thing. And is not Shakespeare's morality, his valor, candor, tolerance, truthfulness; his whole victorious strength and greatness, which can triumph over such obstructions, visible there too? Great as the world! No twisted, poor convex-concave mirror, reflecting all objects with its own convexities and concavities; a perfectly level mirror,—that is to say withal, if we will understand it, a man justly related to all things and men, a good man. It is truly a lordly spectacle how this great soul takes in all kinds of men and objects, a Falstaff, an Othello, a Juliet, a Coriolanus; sets them all forth to us in their round completeness; loving, just, the equal brother of all. 'Novum Organum,' and all the intellect you will find in Bacon, is of a quite secondary order; earthy, material, poor in comparison with this. Among modern men, one finds, in strictness, almost nothing of the same rank. Goethe alone, since the days of Shakespeare, reminds me of it. Of him, too, you say that he saw the object; you may say what he himself says of Shakespeare, 'His characters are like watches with dial-plates of transparent crystal; they show you the hour like others, and the inward mechanism also is all visible.'"

"Dante, for depth of sincerity, is like an antique Prophet, too; his words, like theirs, come from his very heart. One need not wonder if it were predicted that his Poem might be the most enduring thing our Europe has yet made; for nothing so endures as a truly spoken word. All cathedrals, pontificalities, brass and stone, and outer arrangement never so lasting, are brief in comparison to an unfathomable heart-song like this: one feels as if it might survive, still of importance to men, when these had all sunk into new irrecognizable combinations, and had ceased individually to be. Europe has made much; great cities, great empires, encyclopædias, creeds, bodies of opinion and practice: but it has made little of the class of Dante's Thought. Homer yet is, veritably present face to face with every open soul of us; and Greece, where is it? Desolate for thousands of years; away, vanished; a bewildered heap of stones and rubbish, the life and existence of it all gone. Like a dream; like the dust of King Agamemnon! Greece was; Greece, except in the words it spoke, is not."

J. C. Shairp, in his "On Poetic Interpretation of Nature" (p. 19), says:—

"The real nature and intrinsic truth of Poetry will be made more apparent, if we may turn aside for a moment to reflect on the essence of that state of mind which we call poetic, the genesis of that creation which we call Poetry. Whenever any object of sense, or spectacle of the outer world, any truth of reason, or event of past history, any fact of human experience, any moral or spiritual reality; whenever, in short, any fact or object which the sense, or the intellect, or the soul, or the spirit of man can apprehend, comes home to one so as to touch him to the quick, to pierce him with a more than usual vividness and sense of reality, then is awakened that stirring of the imagination, that glow of emotion, in which Poetry is born. There is no truth cognizable by man which may not shape itself into Poetry."

The passages just quoted are but examples of many that might be cited expressing the strength and scope of the poetic spirit, its truth-revealing quality, its penetrating yet comprehensive grasp of the realities. Shelley says, "A poem is the very image of life expressed in its eternal truth"; and Wordsworth that poetry is "the breath and finer spirit of all knowledge." These utterances will hardly be deemed poetical extravagancies to one who has read such things as the Ninetieth Psalm, "King Lear," or "The Deserted Village," or "Elaine."

There is no form of inspiring truth which does not find expression in literature, but it is preëminently a revelation of human life and experience, a proclamation from the housetops of the supreme beauty and excellence of truth and virtue. This brings us close to the question of moral education, and the elements in literature that contribute to this end. Literary critics are quick to take alarm at the propensity of the schoolmaster and the moralist to make literature the vehicle of moral training. To saddle the poets with a moral purpose would be like changing Pegasus into a plough-horse. But the moral quality in the best literature is not something saddled on, it is rather like the frame and muscle which give strength to the body, or, to use a more fitting figure, it is the very pulse and heart-beat of the highest idealism. The proneness toward moralizing, toward formal didacticism, can be best of all corrected by the use of choice literature. The best literature is free from moral pedantry, but full of moral suggestion and stimulus. Edmund Clarence Stedman says, in his "Nature and Elements of Poetry" (p. 216):—

"The highest wisdom—that of ethics—seems closely affiliated with poetic truth. A prosaic moral is injurious to virtue, by making it repulsive. The moment goodness becomes tedious and unideal in a work of art, it is not real goodness; the would-be artist, though a very saint, has mistaken his form of expression. On the other hand, extreme beauty and power in a poem or picture always carry a moral, they are inseparable from a certain ethical standard; while vice suggests a depravity.... An obtrusive moral in poetic form is a fraud on its face, and outlawed of art. But that all great poetry is essentially ethical is plain from any consideration of Homer, Dante, and the best dramatists and lyrists, old and new."

In literature, as in life, those persons make the strongest moral impression who have the least express discussion of morals. Their actions speak, and the moral qualities appear, not in didactic formality and isolation, but in their life setting. This is seen in the great dramas, novels, and epic poems.

These masterpieces are of strong and lasting value to the schools because they bring out human conduct and character in a rich variety of forms corresponding to life. Against the background of scenery created by the poet, men and women and children march along to their varied performances. Theseus, Ulysses, Crusoe, Aladdin, Alfred, Horatius, Cinderella, Portia, Evangeline,—they speak and act before us with all the realism and fidelity to human instincts peculiar to the poet's art. These men and women, who are set in action before us, stir up all our dormant thought-energy. We observe and judge their motives and approve or condemn their actions. We are stirred to sympathy or pity or anger. Such an intense study of motives and conduct, as offered in literature, is like a fresh spring from which well up strengthening waters. The warmth and energy with which judgments are passed upon the deeds of children and adults is the original source of moral ideas. Literature is especially rich in opportunities to register these convictions. It is not the bare knowledge of right and wrong developed, but the deep springs of feeling and emotion are opened, which gush up into volitions and acts.

Just as we form opinions of people from their individual acts, and draw inferences as to their character and motives, so the overt act of Brutus or of Miles Standish stands out so clear against the background of passing events that an unerring judgment falls upon the doer. A single act, seen in its relations, always calls forth such a sentence of good or ill. Whether it be a gentle deed of mercy, or the hammer-stroke that fells a giant or routs an army, as with Charles Martel or Alfred, the sense of right or wrong is the deep underflow that gives meaning to all events and stamps character.

There is, however, a deeper and more intense moral teaching in literature than that which flows from the right or wrong of individual acts. The whole life and evolution of character in a person, if graphically drawn, reveal the principles of conduct and their fruitage. Character is a growth. Deeds are only the outward signs of the direction in which the soul is moving. A dramatist like Shakespeare, or a novelist like George Eliot, gives us a biographical development. Deeds are done which leave their traces. Tendencies are formed which grow into habits, and thus a character ripens steadily toward its reward. We become conscious that certain deeper principles control thought and action, whether good or bad. There is a rule of law, a sort of fatalism, in human life. "The mills of the gods grind slow, but they grind exceeding small." It is the function of the dramatist or novelist to reveal these working principles in conduct. When the principle adopted by the actor is a good one, it works out well-being in spite of misfortunes; when evil, the furies are on the track of the evil-doer. Men do not gather grapes of thorns or figs of thistles. As we move on from step to step in a life-history, the sympathy deepens. The fatal influence of a false step, followed up, is keenly felt by the reader; the upward tendency of a right act inspires and lifts into freedom. But whether we love or hate or pity, the character moves on in the course which his deeds mark out. When finally he is overwhelmed in shame and defeat, we see the early tendencies and later forces which have led to this result. If ethical triumph is achieved, we recognize the reward of generous, unselfish impulses followed out.

As the interest in such a life-history deepens, the lessons it evolves come out with convincing and overwhelming power. The effect of a great novel or drama is more intense and lasting than any sermon. The elements of thought and feeling have been accumulating energy and momentum through all the scenes, and when contracted into a single current at the close they sweep forward with the strength of a river. A masterpiece works at the foundations of our sympathies and moral judgments. To bring ourselves under the spell of a great author and to allow him, hour after hour and perhaps for days in succession, to sway our feelings and rule far up among the sources of our moral judgments, is to give him great opportunity to stamp our character with his convictions. We seldom spend so many hours in close companionship with a living friend as with some master of the art of character-delineation. Children are susceptible to this strong influence. Many of them take easily to books, and many others need but wise direction to bring them under the touch of their formative influence. A book sometimes produces a more lasting effect upon the character and conduct of a child than a close companion. Nor is this true only in the case of book-lovers. It is probable that the great majority of children may feel the wholesome effect of such books if wisely used at the right time. To select a few of the best books as companions to a child, and teach him to love their companionship, is one of the most hopeful things in education. The boy or girl who reads some of our choice epics, stories, novels, dramas, and biographies, allowing the mind to ponder upon the problems of conduct involved, will receive many deep and permanent moral lessons. The realism with which the artist clothes his characters only strengthens the effect and makes them lasting food for thought in the coming years. Even in early childhood we are able to detect what is noble and debasing in conduct as thus graphically and naturally revealed, and a child forms an unerring judgment along moral lines. The best influence that literature has to bestow, therefore, may produce its effect early in tender years, where impressions are deep and permanent. There are many other elements of lasting culture-value in the study of literature, but first of all the deep and permanent truths taught by the classics are those of human life and conduct.

George Willis Cooke gives clear and simple expression to the ethical force in poetry ("Poets and Problems," p. 46):—

"True poetry is for instruction as much as for pleasure, though it inculcate no formal lessons. Right moral teaching is by example far more than by precept; and the real poet teaches through the higher purpose he arouses, by the stimulus he gives, and by the purer motive he awakens. He gives no precept to recite, no homilies to con over, no rules for formal repetition; but he gives the spirit of life and the impulse of true activity. An infallible test of the great poet is that he inspires us with a sense of the richness and grandeur of life."

Rooted in the genuine realism of social life, moral ideas are still more strongly energized by feeling and even by passion. It is doubtful if moral ideas have any roots that do not reach down into deep and genuine feeling.

Ruskin, in "Sesame and Lilies," speaks to the point.

"Having then faithfully listened to the great teachers, that you may enter into their Thoughts, you have yet this higher advance to make,—you have to enter into their Hearts. As you go to them first for clear sight, so you must stay with them that you may share at last their just and mighty Passion. Passion, or "sensation." I am not afraid of the word; still less of the thing. You have heard many outcries against sensation lately; but, I can tell you, it is not less sensation we want, but more. The ennobling difference between one man and another—between one animal and another—is precisely in this, that one feels more than another. If we were sponges, perhaps sensation might not be easily got for us; if we were earthworms, liable at every instant to be cut in two by the spade, perhaps too much sensation might not be good for us. But, being human creatures, it is good for us; nay, we are only human in so far as we are sensitive, and our honor is precisely in proportion to our passion.

"You know I said of that great and pure society of the dead, that it would allow 'no vain or vulgar person to enter there.' What do you think I meant by a 'vulgar' person? What do you yourselves mean by 'vulgarity'? You will find it a fruitful subject of thought; but, briefly, the essence of all vulgarity lies in want of sensation. Simple and innocent vulgarity is merely an untrained and undeveloped bluntness of body and mind; but in true inbred vulgarity, there is a deathful callousness, which, in extremity, becomes capable of every sort of bestial habit and crime, without fear, without pleasure, without horror, and without pity. It is in the blunt hand and the dead heart, in the diseased habit, in the hardened conscience, that men become vulgar; they are forever vulgar, precisely in proportion as they are incapable of sympathy,—of quick understanding,—of all that, in deep insistence on the common, but most accurate term, may be called the 'tact' or touch-faculty of body and soul; that tact which the Mimosa has in trees, which the pure woman has above all creatures,—fineness and fulness of sensation, beyond reason,—the guide and sanctifier of reason itself. Reason can but determine what is true: it is the God-given passion of humanity which alone can recognize what God has made good.

"We come then to the great concourse of the Dead, not merely to know from them what is True, but chiefly to feel with them, what is Righteous. Now to feel with them we must be like them; and none of us can become that without pains. As the true knowledge is disciplined and tested knowledge,—not the first thought that comes,—so the true passion is disciplined and tested passion,—not the first passion that comes."

When we add to this deep feeling and sympathy the versatile poetic imagination which freely constructs all phases of social life and conduct, we have that union of the great powers of the mind and heart which give such concentrated ethical energy to the best literature.

Shelley, in his "Defence of Poetry" (pp. 13-14, 20), says:—

"The whole objection, however, of the immorality of poetry rests upon a misconception of the manner in which poetry acts to produce the moral improvement of man. Ethical science arranges the elements which poetry has created, and propounds schemes and proposes examples of civil and domestic life; nor is it for want of admirable doctrines that men hate, and despise, and censure, and deceive, and subjugate one another. But poetry acts in another and diviner manner. It awakens and enlarges the mind itself by rendering it the receptacle of a thousand unapprehended combinations of thought. Poetry lifts the veil from the hidden beauty of the world, and makes familiar objects be as if they were not familiar; it reproduces all that it represents, and the impersonations clothed in its Elysian light stand thenceforward in the minds of those who have once contemplated them, as memorials of that gentle and exalted content which extends itself over all thoughts and actions with which it coexists. The great secret of morals is love; or a going out of our own nature, and an identification of ourselves with the beautiful which exists in thought, action, or person, not our own. A man, to be greatly good, must imagine intensely and comprehensively; he must put himself in the place of another and of many others; the pains and pleasures of his species must become his own. The great instrument of moral good is the imagination; and poetry administers to the effect by acting upon the cause."

"The drama being that form under which a greater number of modes of expression of poetry are susceptible of being combined than any other, the connection of poetry and social good is more observable in the drama than in whatever other form. And it is indisputable that the highest perfection of human society has ever corresponded with the highest dramatic excellence; and that the corruption or the extinction of the drama in a nation where it has once flourished, is a mark of corruption of manners, and an extinction of the energies which sustain the soul of social life."

The inseparable union of the intellectual, moral, and imaginative elements is well expressed by Shairp in his "On Poetic Interpretation of Nature" (pp. 23-24):—

"Imagination in its essence seems to be, from the first, intellect and feeling blended and interpenetrating each other. Thus it would seem that purely intellectual acts belong to the surface and outside of our nature,—as you pass onward to the depths, the more vital places of the soul, the intellectual, the emotional, and the moral elements are all equally at work, —and this in virtue of their greater reality, their more essential truth, their nearer contact with the centre of things. To this region belong all acts of high imagination—the region intermediate between pure understanding and moral affection, partaking of both elements, looking equally both ways."

Besides the moral element or fundamental truth involved, every classic masterpiece is infused therefore with an element of imagination. Whether in prose or verse, the artist reveals himself in the creative touch. The rich coloring and imagery of his own mind give a tint to every object. The literary artist is never lacking in a certain, perhaps indefinable, charm. He possesses a magic wand that transforms into beauty every commonplace object that is met. We observe this in Irving, Hawthorne, Warner, as well as in still greater literary masters. Our poets, novelists, and essayists must all dip their pens in this magic ink. Even Webster and Burke, Lincoln and Sumner, must rise to the region of fancy if they give their thought sufficient strength of wing to carry it into the coming years. The themes upon which they discoursed kindled the imagination and caused them to break forth into figures of speech and poetic license. The creative fancy is that which gives beauty, picturesqueness, and charm to all the work of poet or novelist. This element of fancy diffuses itself as a living glow through every classic product that was made to endure. In the masters of style the rhythmic flow and energy of language are enlivened by poetic imagery. Figures of speech in architectural simplicity and chasteness stand out to symbolize thought. That keenness and originality which astonishes us in master thinkers is due to the magic vigor and picturesqueness of their images. Underneath and permeating all this wealth of ideas is the versatile and original mind which sees everything in the glow of its own poetic temperament, kindling the susceptible reader to like inspiration. Among literary masters this creative power shows itself in an infinite variety of forms, pours itself through a hundred divergent channels, and links itself so closely with the individuality of the writer as to merge imperceptibly into his character and style. But as we cannot secure wholesome bread without yeast, so we shall fail of a classic without imagination.

Stedman says: "If anything great has been achieved without exercise of the imagination, I do not know it. I am referring to striking productions and achievements, not to acts of virtue. Nevertheless, at the last analysis, it might be found that imagination has impelled even the saints and martyrs of humanity. Imagination is the creative origin of what is fine, not in art and song alone, but also in all forms of action—in campaigns, civil triumphs, material conquest. I have mentioned its indispensability to the scientists." He says further: "Yet if there is one gift which sets Shakespeare at a distance even from those who approach him on one or another side, it is that of his imagination. As he is the chief of poets, we infer that the faculty in which he is supereminent must be the greatest of poetic endowments. Yes: in his wonderland, as elsewhere, imagination is king."

Not only is it true that the vitality of poets and prose writers, the conceptive power of scientists, inventors, and business organizers, depend upon the fertility and strength of the imagination, but throughout the broader reaches of common humanity this power is everywhere present—constructive and creative. Max Müller has shown that the root words of language are imbedded in metaphor, that "Language is fossil poetry." Again, the mythologies of the different races, grand and stately, or fair and lovely, are the immediate product of the folk mind.

It has been said that "The man of culture is preëminently a man of imagination." But the kind of mental alertness, freedom, and joy which is suggested by the term *culture* may spring up in the heart of every boy and girl endowed with a modicum of human nature. Hamilton Wright Mabie, in his "Books and Culture" (pp. 148-149), says:—

"The development of the imagination, upon the power of which both absorption of knowledge and creative capacity depend, is, therefore, a matter of supreme importance. To this necessity educators will some day open their eyes, and educational systems will some day conform; meantime, it must be done mainly by individual work. Knowledge, discipline, and technical training of the best sort are accessible on every hand; but the development of the faculty which unites all these in the highest form of activity must be secured mainly by personal effort. The richest and most accessible material for this highest education is furnished by art; and the form of art within reach of every civilized man, at all times, in all places, is the book. To these masterpieces, which have been called the books of life, all men may turn with the assurance that as the supreme achievements of the imagination they have the power of awakening, stimulating, and enriching it in the highest degree."

Besides the strong thread of truth and the work of the swift-glancing shuttle of imagination, the woven fabric of the literary master must show a beauteous pattern or form. The melody and music of poetry spring from a rhythmic form. Apparently stiff and formal, it is yet the consensus of critics that only through this channel can the soul of truth and beauty escape from the poet, and manifest itself to others. Says George Willis Cooke, "The poet worships at the triple shrine of beauty, love, and truth; and his mission is to teach men that all other objects and places of veneration are but faint imitations of this one form of faith." But the spirit of this worship can best embody itself in the poetic form.

Schlegel, in his "Dramatic Art and Literature" (p. 340), says:—

"The works of genius cannot therefore be permitted to be without form; but of this there is no danger.... [Some] critics ... interpret it [form] merely in a mechanical, and not in an organical sense.... Organical form, again, is innate; it unfolds itself from within, and acquires its determination contemporaneously with the perfect development of the germ. We everywhere discover such forms in nature throughout the whole range of living powers, from the crystallization of salts and minerals to plants and flowers, and from these again to the human body. In the fine arts, as well as in the domain of nature,—the supreme artist,—all genuine forms are organical, that is, determined by the quality of the work. In a word, the form is nothing but a significant exterior, the speaking physiognomy of each thing, which, as long as it is not disfigured by any destructive accident, gives a true evidence of its hidden essence."

Some products, like the "Paradise Lost," "Thanatopsis," and "Hamlet," show such a perfect fitness of form to thought that every effort to change or modify is profanation. The classic form and thought go together. As far as possible, therefore, it is desirable to leave these creations in their native strength, and not to mar the work of masters. The poet has moulded his thought and feeling into these forms and transfused them with his own imagery and individuality. The power of the writer is in his peculiar mingling of the poetic elements. Our English and American classics, therefore, should be read in their original form as far as possible.

A fixed form is not always necessary. We need many of the stories and epics that were written in other languages. Fortunately some of the works of the old poets are capable of taking on a new dress. The story of Ulysses has been told in verse and prose, in translation, paraphrase, and simple narrative for children. Much, indeed of the old beauty and original strength of the poem is lost in all these renderings; but the central truths which give the poetic work its persistent value are still retained. Such a poem is like a person; the underlying thought, though dressed up by different persons with varying taste and skill, is yet the same; the same heart beats beneath the kingly robes and the peasant's frock. Robinson Crusoe has had many renderings, but remains the same old story in spite of variations. The Bible has been translated into all modern tongues, but it is a classic in each. The Germans claim they have as good a Shakespeare as we.

But many of the best masterpieces were originally written in other languages, and to be of use to us the ancient form of thought must be broken. The spirit of the old masters must be poured into new moulds. In educating our children we need the stories of Bellerophon, Perseus, Hercules, Rustum, Tell, Siegfried, Virginius, Roland, Wallace, King Arthur. Happily some of the best modern writers have come to our help. Walter Scott, Macaulay, Dickens, Kingsley, Hawthorne, Irving, and Arnold have gathered up the old wine and poured it into new bottles. They have told the old stories in simple Anglo-Saxon for the boys and girls of our homes and schools. Nor are these renderings of the old masters lacking in that element of fancy and vigor of expression which distinguishes fertile writers. They have entered freely and fondly into the old spirit, and have allowed it to pour itself copiously through these modern channels. It takes a poet, in fact, to modernize an ancient story. There are, indeed, many renderings of the old stories which are not ideal, which, however, we sometimes use for lack of anything better.

From the preceding discussion we may conclude that a choice piece of literature must embody a lasting truth, reveal the permeating glow of an artist's imagination, and find expression in some form of beauty. But these elements are so mingled and interlaced, so organically grown into one living plant, that even the critics have given up the effort to dissect and isolate them.

There are other strength-conferring qualities in good literature which will be discussed more fully in those chapters which deal with the particular literary materials selected for use in the schools.

Among the topics to be treated in connection with materials which illustrate them, are the following: the strong handling of essential historical ideas in literature; the best novel and drama, as sources and means of culture; religious ideals as embodied in the choicest forms of literature; the powerful patriotic and social influence of the best writers; the educative quality of the humorous phases of literature; the great writers as models of skill and enthusiasm in teaching.

In the foregoing pages the significance of literature among great studies has been but briefly and inadequately suggested by these few quotations and comments. It would be easy to multiply similar testimony from the most competent judges. But enough has been said to remind teachers of this rich treasure house of educative materials. Those teachers who wish to probe deeper into this subject will find that it has been handled in a masterly way by some of the great essayists and critics. We will suggest the following for more elaborate study:—

Ruskin's "Sesame and Lilies." The power and charm of Ruskin's writing appears in full measure in these essays.

Carlyle's "Heroes and Hero Worship," especially the chapters on "The Hero as Poet," and "The Hero as Man of Letters."

Shelley's "Defence of Poetry" (edited by Cook, and published by Ginn & Co.) is a literary masterpiece of rare beauty and charm.

Emerson's "Essay on History."

George Willis Cooke, "Poets and Problems" (Houghton, Mifflin, & Co.). The first chapter, "The Poet as Teacher," is very suggestive, while the chapters on Tennyson, Ruskin, and Browning are fine introductions for those who will study the authors themselves.

"The Book Lover," James Baldwin (McClurg & Co.).

Charles Kingsley's "Literary and General Essays" (Macmillan & Co.). Chapter on "English Literature," and others.

Scudder's "Literature in Schools" (Houghton, Mifflin, & Co.). Excellent for teachers.

J. C. Shairp, "On Poetic Interpretation of Nature" (Houghton, Mifflin, & Co.).

Matthew Arnold's "Sweetness and Light."

Lowell's "Books and Libraries" (Houghton, Mifflin, & Co.).

Edmund Clarence Stedman's "The Nature and Elements of Poetry" (Houghton, Mifflin, & Co.).

It is not implied that even the essays of critics on the merits of literature can take the place of a study of the works of the best writers.

CHAPTER II

THE USE OF MASTERPIECES AS WHOLES

With the increasing tendency to consider the literary quality and fitness of the reading matter used in our schools, longer poems and stories, like "Snow Bound," "Rip Van Winkle," "Hiawatha," "Aladdin," "The Courtship of Miles Standish," "The Great Stone Face," and even "Lady of the Lake" and "Julius Cæsar," are read and studied as complete wholes. Many of the books now used as readers are not collections of short selections and extracts, as formerly, but editions of single poems, or kindred groups, like "Sohrab and Rustum," or the "Arabian Nights," or "Gulliver's Travels," or a collection of a few complete stories or poems of a single author, as Hawthorne's "Stories of the White Hills," or Lowell's "Vision of Sir Launfal," and other poems. Even the regular series of readers are often made up largely of longer poems and prose masterpieces.

The significance of this change is the deeper regard which is being paid to good literature as a strong agency of true culture. The real thought and the whole thought of the best authors is sought for, presupposing, of course, that they are within the range of the children's comprehension. The reading books of a generation ago contained oftentimes just as choice literary materials as now; but the chief purpose of its selection was to give varied exercise in oral reading, not to cultivate a taste for good literature by furnishing complete poetic and prose specimens for full and enthusiastic study. The teachers who lay stress on elocutionary skill are not quite satisfied with this drift toward literary study as such. It remains to be seen how both aims, good oral rendering and superior literary training, can be secured at the same time.

At the close of the last chapter of this volume we give a carefully selected series of the literary materials adapted to the different grades. This body of selections, taken from a wide range of literature, will constitute a basis for our whole treatise. Having made plain by our previous discussion what we understand by the quality of literary masterpieces, we will next consider why these poems and stories should be read and studied as complete wholes, not by fragments or by extracts, but as whole works of literary art.

1. A stronger interest is developed by the study, for several weeks, of a longer complete masterpiece. The interest grows as we move into such a story or poem as "Sohrab and Rustum." A longer and closer acquaintance with the characters represented produces a stronger personal sympathy, as in the case of Cordelia in "King Lear," or of Silas Marner. The time usually spent in school upon some classic fragment or selection is barely sufficient to start up an interest. It does not bring us past the threshold of a work of art. We drop it just at the point where the momentum of interest begins to show itself. Think of the full story of Aladdin or Crusoe or Ulysses. Take an extract from "Lady of the Lake," "Rip Van Winkle," "Evangeline." The usual three or four pages given in the reader, even if taken from the first part, would scarcely suffice to bring the children into the movement of the story; but oftentimes the fragment is extracted from the body of the play without preliminary or sequence. In reading a novel, story, or poem, we do not begin to feel strongly this interest till two or three chapters are passed. Then it begins to deepen, the plot thickens, and a desire springs up to follow out the fortune of the characters. We become interested in the persons, and our thoughts are busy with them in the midst of other employments or in leisure moments. The personality of the hero takes hold of us as that of an intimate friend. Such an interest, gradually awakened and deepened as we move into the comprehension of a work of art, is the open sesame to all the riches of an author's storehouse of thought.

This kind of interest presupposes in the children the ability to appreciate and enjoy the thought, and even the style, of the author. Interest in this sense is a fundamental test of the suitableness of the story or poem to lay hold of the inner life of the children. In many cases there will be difficulties at the outset in awakening this genuine form of interest, but if the selection is appropriate, the preparation and skill of the teacher will be equal to its accomplishment.

As we get deeper into the study of masterpieces, we shall discover that there are stronger and deepening sources of a genuine interest. Even the difficulties and problems which are supposed to dampen interest will be found, with proper study, to be the source of a stronger appreciation and enthusiasm. The refining and strengthening of these interests in literature leads on steadily to the final goal of study, a cultivated taste and habit of using the best books.

2. A complete work of a master writer is a unit of thought. It is almost as complete a whole as a living organism. Its parts, like the branches of a tree, have no vitality except in communication with the living trunk. In the "Vision of Sir Launfal," there is a single thought, like a golden thread, running through the poem, which gives unity and perfection to it. The separate parts of the poem have very great intrinsic beauty and charm, but their deeper and more vital relation is to this central thought. The story of "The Great Stone Face" is the grouping of a series of interesting episodes along the path of a single developing motive in the life of Ernest. A great writer would scarcely waste his time in trying to produce a work of art without a controlling motive, collecting his thought, as it were, around a vacuum. This hub-thought must become the centre of all intelligent study. The effort to unravel the motive of the author is the deeper stimulus of thoughtful work by both teacher and pupils.

In other studies, like geography, history, and natural science, we are gradually picking out the important units of study, the centres of thought and interest, the types. This effort to escape from the wilderness of jumbled and fractional details into the sunlit region of controlling ideas, is a substantial sign of progress in the teacher's work. In literature these units have been already wrought out into perfect wholes by first-class thinkers.

In the greatest of all studies, the works of the literary masters, we have the surest models of inspiring thought, organized and focussed upon essential topics. Teachers, in some cases, are so little accustomed to lift their heads above the tall grass and weeds around them, that they are overtaken by surprise and bewilderment when called upon to take broad and liberal surveys of the topography of school studies.

It is fortunate that we have, within the fenced boundaries of the commonly recognized school course, these shining specimens of organized, and, what we might call, intelligent thought.

We can set the children at work digging for the root-thoughts of those who are the masters of strong thinking. This digging process is not wholly out of place with children. Their abundant energy can be turned to digging if there is anything worth digging for. Ruskin, in "Sesame and Lilies," says:—

"And it is just the same with men's best wisdom. When you come to a good book, you must ask yourself: 'Am I inclined to work as an Australian miner would? Are my pickaxes and shovels in good order, and am I in good trim myself, my sleeves well up to the elbow, and my breath good, and my temper?' And, keeping the figure a little longer, even at cost of tiresomeness, for it is a thoroughly useful one, the metal you are in search of, being the author's mind or meaning, his words are as the rock which you have to crush and smelt in order to get at it. And your pickaxes are your own care, wit and learning; your smelting furnace is your own thoughtful soul. Do not hope to get at any good author's meaning without those tools and that fire; often you will need sharpest, finest chiselling, and patientest fusing, before you can gather one grain of the metal."

It is not the dreamy, hammock-soothing, vacation idling with pleasant stories that we are now considering. This happy lotus-land has also its fitting season, in the sultry heats of summer, when tired people put their minds out to grass. Any study will grow dull and sleepy that lacks energy.

Teachers who shrink back with anxiety lest works such as Irving's "Sketch Book," "Evangeline," "Merchant of Venice," and "Marmion," are too hard for children in sixth, seventh, and eighth grades, should consider for a moment what classical preparatory schools for centuries have required of boys from ten to twelve years of age, the study of "Cæsar," "Eutropius," and "Virgil," of "Herodotus" and "Xenophon," in unknown languages extremely difficult to master. Yet it has been claimed for ages, by the best scholars, that this was the true strength-producing discipline for boys. It would hardly be extravagant to say that the masterpieces of literature now used, in our intermediate and grammar grades, are not a quarter so difficult and four times as appropriate and interesting as the Latin and Greek authors just cited. It seems obvious that we are summoned to a more energetic study and treatment of our masterpieces.

This struggle to get at the deeper undercurrent of thought in an author is the true stimulus and discipline of such studies.

A great author approaches his deeper thought step by step. He has many side-lights, variety of episode and preliminary. He provides for the proper scenery and setting for his thought. He does not bring us at once, point blank, upon his hero or upon the hero's fate. There is great variety of inference and suggestion in the preparation and grouping of the artist's work. As in climbing some mountain peak, we wind through cañon, along rugged hillsides and spurs, only now and then catching a glimpse of the towering object of our climb, reaching, after many a devious and toilsome march, the rugged backbone of the giant; so the poet carries us along many a winding road, through byways and thickets, over hill and plain, before he brings us into full view of the main object of search. But after awhile we do stand face to face with a real character, and are conscious of the framework upon which it is built. King Saul has run his course and is about to reap the reward of his doings, to lie down in the bed which he has prepared. We see the author's deeper plan, and realize that his characters act along the line of the silent but invincible laws of social life and conduct. These deep significant truths of human experience do not lie upon the surface. If we are really to get a deep insight into human character, as portrayed by the masters, we must not be in haste. We should be willing to follow our guide patiently and await results.

A complete masterpiece, studied as a whole, reveals the author's power. It gives some adequate perception of his style and compass. A play, a poem, a novel, a biography, is a unit. No single part can give a satisfactory idea of the whole. A single scene from "Crusoe" or from the "Merchant of Venice" does not give us the author's meaning. An extract from one of Burke's speeches supplies no adequate notion of his statesmanlike grasp of thought. To get some impression of what Daniel Webster was we must read a whole speech. A literary product is like a masterpiece of architecture. The whole must stand out in the due proportion of its parts to reveal the master's thought.

"Walk about Zion, and go round about her:
Tell the towers thereof.
Mark ye well her bulwarks, consider her palaces;
That ye may tell it to the generations following."

To have read through with care and thoughtful appreciation a single literary masterpiece and to have felt the full measure of a master's power, is a rare and lasting stroke of culture. As children move up through the grades they may receive the strong and abiding impress of the masters of style. Let it come to them in its undiminished strength. To feel the powerful tonic effect of the best stories and poems suited to their age will give them such an appreciation of what is genuine and good in literature, that frivolous and trashy reading is measured at its true value.

The fragments and extracts with which our higher readers are filled are not without power and influence upon culture. They have given many children their first taste of the beauty and strength of literature. But it is a great mistake to tear these gems of thought from their setting in literature and life, and to jam them into the close and crowded quarters of a text-book. Why satisfy ourselves with crumbs and fragments when a full rich feast may be had for the asking?

In some cases it is said that the reading of fragments of large poems or plays has excited curiosity and led to the reading of the larger wholes. This is doubtless true, but in the greater number of cases we are inclined to think the habit of being satisfied with fragments has checked the formation of any appreciation of literary wholes. This tendency to be satisfied with piecemeal performances illustrates painfully the shallowness and incoherency of much of our educational work. If teachers cannot think beyond a broken page of Shakespeare, why should children burden themselves with the labor of thought? Charles Kingsley, in his essay on English literature, says:—

"But I must plead for whole works. 'Extracts' and 'Select Beauties' are about as practical as the worthy in the old story, who, wishing to sell his house, brought one of the bricks to market as a specimen. It is equally unfair on the author and on the pupil; for it is impossible to show the merits or demerits of a work of art, even to explain the truth or falsehood of any particular passage, except by viewing the book as an organic whole."

What would the authors themselves say upon seeing their work thus mutilated? There is even a touch of the farcical in the effort to read naturally and forcibly and discuss intelligently a fragment like Antony's speech over Cæsar.

3. The moral effect of a complete masterpiece is deeper and more permanent. Not only do we see a person acting in more situations, revealing thus his motives and hidden springs of action, but the thread of his thought and life is unravelled in a steady sequence. Later acts are seen as the result of former tendencies. The silent reign of moral law in human actions is discovered. Slowly but surely conduct works out its own reward along the line of these deeper principles of action. Even in the books read in the early grades these profound lessons of life come out clear and strong. Robinson Crusoe, Theseus, Siegfried, Hiawatha, Beauty and the Beast, Jason, King Arthur, and Ulysses are not holiday guests. They are face to face with the serious problems of life. Each person is seen in the present make-up and tendency of his character. When the eventual wind-up comes, be it a collapse or an ascension, we see how surely and fatally such results spring from such motives and tendencies. Washington is found to be the first in the hearts of his countrymen; Arnold is execrated; King Lear moves on blindly to the reward which his own folly has prearranged; Macbeth entangles himself in a network of fatal errors; Adam Bede emerges from the bitter ordeal of disappointment with his manly qualities subdued but stronger. Give the novelist or poet time and opportunity, and he is the true interpreter of conduct and destiny. He reveals in real and yet ideal characters the working out in life of the fundamental principles of moral action.

4. A classic work is often a picture of an age, a panoramic survey of an historical epoch. Scott's "Marmion" is such a graphic and dramatic portrayal of feudalism in Scotland. The castle with its lord, attendants, and household, the steep frowning walls and turrets, the moat, drawbridge, and dungeon, the chapel, halls, and feastings, the knight clad in armor, on horseback with squire and troop,—these are the details of the first picture. The cloister and nuns, with their sequestered habits and dress, their devotion and masses, supply the other characteristic picture of that age,

with Rome in the background. The court scene and ball in King James's palace, before the day of Flodden, the view of Scotland's army from the mountain side, with the motley hordes from highland and lowland and neighboring isles, and lastly, the battle of Flodden itself, where wisdom is weighed and valor put to the final test,—all these are but the parts of a well-adjusted picture of life in feudal times on the Scottish border. There is incidental to the narrative much vivid description of Scotch scenery and geography, of mountain or valley, of frowning castle or rocky coast, much of Scotch tradition, custom, superstition, and clannishness. The scenes in cloister and dungeon and on the battle-field are more intensely real than historical narratives can be. While not strict history, this is truer than history because it brings us closer to the spirit of that time. Marmion and Douglas stand out more clear and lifelike than the men of history.

Although feudalism underwent constant changes and modifications in every country of Europe, it is still true that "Marmion" is a type of feudal conditions, not only in Scotland, but in other parts of Europe, and a full perception of Scott's poem will make one at home in any part of European history during feudal times. As a historical picture of life, it is a key to the spirit and animating ideas that swayed the Western nations during several centuries. It is fiction, not history, in the usual sense, and yet it gives a more real and vivid consciousness of the forces at work in that age than history proper.

While the plot of the story covers a narrow field, only a few days of time and a small area of country, its roots go deep into the whole social, religious, and political fabric of that time. It touches real history at a critical point in the relations between England and Scotland. It is stirred also by the spirit of the Scotch bard and of minstrelsy. It shows what a hold Rome had in those days, even in the highlands of Scotland. It is full of Scotch scenery and geography. It rings with the clarion of war and of battle. It reveals the contempt in which letters were held even by the most powerful nobles. Oxen are described as drawing cannon upon the field of Flodden, and in time these guns broke down the walls of feudalism. As a historical picture Marmion is many-sided, and the roots of the story reach out through the whole fabric of society, showing how all the parts cohere. Such a piece of historical literature may serve as a centre around which to gather much and varied information through other school and home readings. Children may find time to read "Ivanhoe," "The Crusades," "Roland," "Don Quixote," "The Golden Legend," "Macbeth," "Goetz von Berlichingen," etc. They will have a nucleus upon which to gather many related facts and ideas. It should also be brought into proper connection with the regular lessons in history and geography. History reveals itself to the poet in these wonderfully vivid and lifelike types. In many of these historical poems, as "William Tell," "Evangeline," "Crusoe," "The Nibelung Song," "Miles Standish," the "Odyssey," "Sohrab and Rustum," some hero stands in the centre of the narrative, and can be understood as a representative figure of his times only as the whole series of events in his life is unrolled.

Where the study of larger literary wholes has been taken up in good faith, it has brought a rich blessing of intelligent enthusiasm. Even in primary schools, where literary wholes like "Hiawatha," "Robinson Crusoe," and the "Golden Touch" are handled with a view to exploit their whole content, there has been a remarkable enrichment of the whole life of the children. Such a treatment has gone so deep into the problems and struggling conditions of life delineated, that the children have become occupied with the tent-making, boat-building, spinning, and various constructions incident to the development of the story.

5. If it is true, as clearly expressed by strong thinkers in the most various fields of deeper investigation, that many of the chief literary products that have come down to us from former ages are the only means by which we can be brought into vital touch and sympathy with the spirit and motives then ruling among men; if it is equally true that children will not grow up to the proper appreciation and interpretation of our present life, except as they have experienced, in thought and interest at least, the chief struggles and motives of our fathers,—we may find in these historic and literary materials the deep and living springs of true education for children.

The thought of the educative power of this ancestral literature has been forcibly expressed by many eminent writers.

Scudder, in "Literature in School," says:—

"There is the element of continuity. In the Roman household there stood the cinerary urns which held the ashes of the ancestors of the family. Do you think the young ever forgot the unbroken line of descent by which they climbed to the heroic founders of the state? In the Jewish family the child was taught to think and speak of the God of Abraham, and of Isaac, and of Jacob. In that great succession he heard a voice which told him his nation was not of a day. It is the business of the old to transmit to the young the great traditions of the past of the country; to feed anew the undying flame of patriotism.

"It is this concentration in poetry and the more lofty prose which gives to literary art its preciousness as a symbol of human endeavor, and renders it the one essential and most serviceable means for keeping alive the smouldering coals of patriotism. It is the torch passed from one hand to another, signaling hope and warning; and the one place above all others where its light should be kindled is where the young meet together, in those American temples which the people have built in every town and village in the country."

Mabie, in "Books and Culture" (pp. 88, 89-113), says:—

"Now, it is upon this imperishable food which the past has stored up through the genius of great artists that later generations feed and nourish themselves. It is through intimate contact with these fundamental conceptions, worked out with such infinite pain and patience, that the individual experience is broadened to include the experience of the race."

"The student of literature, therefore, finds in its noblest works not only the ultimate results of race experience and the characteristic quality of race genius, but the highest activity of the greatest minds in their happiest and most expansive moments. In this commingling of the best that is in the race and the best that is in the individual, lies the mystery of that double revelation which makes every work of art a disclosure, not only of the nature of the man behind it, but of all men behind him. In this commingling, too, is preserved the most precious deposit of what the race has been and done, and of what the man has seen, felt, and known. In the nature of things no educational material can be richer, none so fundamentally expansive and illuminative."

Emerson, in his "Essay on History," says:—

"The advancing man discovers how deep a property he has in literature, —in all fable as well as in all history. He finds that the poet was no odd fellow who described strange and impossible situations, but that universal man wrote by his pen a confession true for one and true for all. His own secret biography he finds in lines wonderfully intelligible to him, dotted down before he was born. One after another he comes up in his private adventures with every fable of Æsop, of Homer, of Hafiz, of Ariosto, of Chaucer, of Scott, and verifies them with his own head and hands.

"The beautiful fables of the Greeks, being proper creations of the imagination and not of the fancy, are universal verities. What a range of meanings and what perpetual pertinence has the story of Prometheus! Besides its primary value as the first chapter of the history of Europe (the mythology thinly veiling authentic facts, the invention of the mechanic arts and the migration of colonies), it gives the history of religion with some closeness to the faith of later ages."

"Thus in all ways does the soul concentrate and reproduce its treasures for each pupil. He, too, shall pass through the whole cycle of experience. He shall collect into a focus the rays of nature. History no longer shall be a dull book. It shall walk incarnate in every just and wise man. You shall not tell me by languages and titles a catalogue of the volumes you have read. You shall make me feel what periods you have lived. A man shall be the Temple of Fame. He shall walk, as the poets have described that goddess, in a robe painted all over with wonderful events and experiences; his own form and features by their exalted intelligence shall be that variegated vest. I shall find in him the Foreworld; in his childhood the Age of Gold; the Apples of Knowledge; the Argonautic Expedition; the calling of Abraham; the building of the Temple; the Advent of Christ; Dark Ages; the Revival of Letters; the Reformation; the discovery of new lands; the opening of new sciences, and new regions in man."

6. It is not intended to limit the reading of the schools to the longer classics, such as "Snow-Bound," "The Vision of Sir Launfal," and Webster's Bunker Hill speech, etc. There are also many shorter poems and stories, ballads, and myths, that are equally good and stand out as strong, complete expressions of thought such as Tennyson's "Brook," Longfellow's "Village Blacksmith," Whittier's "Barefoot Boy," and many others. These shorter

pieces should be interspersed among the longer, and freely used to give greater variety and zest to reading exercises. Many of the finest literary products of the language are found in these shorter poems and stories. They also should be studied for the beauty and unity of thought contained in each.

7. But the *sustained power* gained from the full and rich study of longer classics is the best fruitage of the reading work. Every term of school should lead the children into the full appreciation of one or more of these masterly works. The value of such study is well expressed by Scudder in his "Literature in Schools" (pp. 54-56):—

"The real point of practical reform, however, is not in the preference of American authors to English, but in the careful concentration of the minds of boys and girls upon standard American literature, in opposition to a dissipation over a desultory and mechanical acquaintance with scraps from a variety of sources, good, bad, and indifferent. In my paper on 'Nursery Classics in School,' I argued that there is a true economy in substituting the great books of that portion of the world's literature which represents the childhood of the world's mind for the thin, quickly forgotten, feeble imaginations of insignificant bookmakers. There is an equally noble economy in engaging the child's mind, when it is passing out of an immature state into one of rational, intelligent appropriation of literature, upon such carefully chosen classic work as shall invigorate and deepen it. There is plenty of vagrancy in reading; the public libraries and cheap papers are abundantly able to satisfy the truant: but it ought to be recognized once for all that the schools are to train the mind into appreciation of literature, not to amuse it with idle diversion; to this end, the simplest and most direct method is to place before boys and girls for their regular task in reading, not scraps from this and that author, duly paragraphed and numbered, but a wisely selected series of works by men whom their country honors, and who have made their country worth living in.

"The continuous reading of a classic is in itself a liberal education; the fragmentary reading of commonplace lessons in minor morals, such as make up much of our reading-books, is a pitiful waste of growing mental powers. Even were our reading-books composed of choice selections from the highest literature, they would still miss the very great advantage which follows upon the steady growth of acquaintance with a sustained piece of literary art. I do not insist, of course, that 'Evangeline' should be read at one session of the school, though it would be exceedingly helpful in training the powers of the mind if, after this poem had been read day by day for a few weeks, it were to be taken up first in its separate thirds, and then in an entire reading. What I claim is that the boy or girl who has read 'Evangeline' through steadily has acquired a certain power in appropriating literature which is not to be had by reading a collection of minor poems,—the power of long-sustained attention and interest."

8. The study of literary wholes, whether longer or shorter, in the common school is based upon the notion that the full, rich thought of the author is the absorbing purpose of our effort. Literature is a reservoir of mental refinement and riches, for the gaining of which we can afford to sacrifice many things and make many even good things subordinate. The words of the wise man in recommending wisdom to the sons of men are not inappropriate: "Hear; for I will speak of excellent things and the opening of my lips shall be right things, and wickedness is an abomination to my lips. Receive my instruction and not silver; and knowledge rather than choice gold. For wisdom is better than rubies; and all the things that may be desired are not to be compared to it."

To get at the wisdom of the best thinkers of the world, so far as it is accessible to children, is the straightforward aim of such study. The teachers of reading, if they but realized it, are the guardians of a temple more beautiful than the Parthenon in the days of Pericles, more impressive than the sacred towers and porticos at Jerusalem; they are the custodians of a treasure far more rich and lasting than that in any palace of a king. Such comparisons, indeed, are almost belittling to the dignity of our subject. How noble and vast is the temple of literature! What single mind can grasp its proportions or the boundless beauty of its decorations? Moreover, it is a living temple, ever springing up afresh, in all its pristine strength and beauty, whereever minds are found reverent, studious, and thoughtful.

9. The old proverb suggests that we "beware of the man of one book," and is significant of a strong practical truth. Our modern life demands a somewhat broader basis of operations than one book can furnish. But a few of the great books, well mastered, give the main elements of strength.

Mabie has a short chapter on the "Books of Life" which "include the original, creative, first-hand books in all literatures, and constitute in the last analysis a comparatively small group, with which any student can thoroughly familiarize himself. The literary impulse of the race has expressed itself in a great variety of works of varying charm and power, but the books which are fountain-heads of vitality, ideas, and beauty are few in number."

The effect upon the teacher of the study of a few of the "Books of Life" is deserving of emphasis. First, by limiting the choice to a few things, teachers are able, without burdening themselves, to penetrate into the deeper thought and meaning of standard works which are good specimens and criteria of all superior literature. Teachers are enabled thus to become, in a limited way, real students of literature. It has been observed, not seldom, that teachers of usual capacity, when turned into a single rich field like that of "Hiawatha" or the "Merchant of Venice" or "The Lays of Ancient Rome" or the "Lady of the Lake," receive an awakening which means much for their general culture and teaching power. The scattering of the attention over miscellaneous selections and fragments can hardly produce this awakening.

Certain difficulties are incident to the reading of longer works as wholes which it is well to recognize.

1. There is no such nice grading of verbal and language difficulties as has been wrought out in some of the standard readers. On this point Scudder says (p. 41 of "Literature in Schools"):—

"The drawback to the use of these nursery classics in the schoolroom undoubtedly has been in the absence of versions which are intelligible to children of the proper age, reading by themselves. The makers of the graded reading-books have expended all their ingenuity in grading the ascent. They have been so concerned about the gradual enlargement of their vocabularies that they have paid slight attention to the ideas which the words were intended to convey. But just this gradation may be secured through the use of these stories, and it only needs that they should be written out in a form as simple, especially as regards the order of words, as that which obtains in the reading-books of equivalent grade."

But in the longer classics for more advanced grades there can be no such adaptation, and the author's form should be retained. The authors of "Rip Van Winkle" or "Snow-Bound" or "Horatius at the Bridge" were not trying to phrase their thought to meet the needs of children, but wrote as the spirit moved them. The greater vigor and intensity of the author's style will make up, however, in large part, for this defect in easy grading. Children are not so much afraid of big or new words, if there is attractiveness and power of thought. The larger richness and variety of language in a fruitful author is a positive advantage as compared with the leanness and dulness of many a smoothly graded reading lesson.

2. It is claimed that there is, in some masterpieces, like "Evangeline" or one of Webster's speeches, a monotony and tiresome sameness which grows burdensome to pupils ere the conclusion is reached. At least there is much less variety in style and thought than in an equal number of pages in the usual reader.

In some cases there is good ground for this criticism. It may be a defect in the writer's style, or in not finding a suitable selection for the class. In some cases it is due to lack of power in the teacher to bring the children properly into close contact with the author's thought.

But dulness and apathy are often found in reading short selections as well as in longer ones. Generally speaking, longer pieces are apt to kindle a deeper and stronger interest. Many of the longer selections have also great variety of rhetorical style. Dickens's "Christmas Carol" is employed in one of the drill books in reading to illustrate all phases of voice and tone.

3. It is not an unusual experience to find that a longer story or poem seems too hard for a class, and it may be impossible to interest them because of verbal or thought difficulties. But the teacher should not give up the struggle at once. Often, in a new author, difficulties that seem at first insurmountable give way before vigorous effort, and a lively interest is awakened. This has been noticed in Macaulay's "Lays of Ancient Rome," in Irving's "Rip Van Winkle," in Scott's "Lady of the Lake," also in Webster's "Speech in reply to Hayne." The teacher should not depend wholly upon the author's making himself intelligible and interesting to the children. His own enthusiasm, clear grasp of thought, suggestive assignment of lesson, and

skill in comment and question should awaken insight and attention. It is advisable at times to pass by specially difficult passages, or leave them for later special study.

4. In some schools it is not possible to secure books containing the complete classics. But even the regular readers often contain complete poems and stories, and several of the large companies are publishing many of the complete masterpieces in good print and binding, no more expensive than the regular readers.

5. The greatest difficulty, after all, is the lack of experience of many teachers with the longer classics. In many cases their inability to select what would suit their classes is a hindrance. But the experience of many teachers with these materials is rapidly settling the question as to the place and importance of the leading masterpieces as well as of many shorter selections.

CHAPTER III

LITERARY MATERIALS FOR THE FIVE UPPER GRADES

There is great abundance and variety of choice reading matter suitable for the grades from the fourth to the eighth inclusive. The best sets of reading-books have drawn from this rich material, but no series of readers can compass adequately the field. Some of the longer classical stories and poems have been incorporated into readers, but a single set of readers cannot be made large enough to contain a quarter of the valuable reading matter which should be furnished in these grades. The large publishing houses now supply, at moderate expense, in small and convenient book form, a great variety of the very best complete masterpieces. In order to show more clearly the richness and variety of this material, we will discuss briefly the principal kinds of reading matter which are distributed through these five grades. We assume that during the first three years of school life children have learned how to read, having mastered the forms and symbols of printed language. At the beginning of the fourth grade, therefore, they are prepared to read some of those choice literary products which constitute a part of the permanent literature of the world. After having collected and arranged these products, we find that they fall into several distinctly marked classes.

1. The Myths.

These include such stories as Hawthorne's "Wonder Book" and "Tanglewood Tales," Peabody's "Old Greek Folk Stories," Kingsley's "Greek Heroes," "The Story of Ulysses," Bryant's translation of the "Iliad" and "Odyssey," Pope's "Homer," and many other prose and poetic renderings of the Greek myths.

Another group of myths include Mabie's "Norse Stories," "Heroes of Asgard," "Siegfried," "Myths of Northern Lands," Skinner's "Readings in Folk Lore," and many forms of the Norse myths. The story of "Hiawatha" belongs also to this group, while some of the earlier English and Roman myths belong to the same class.

The choicest of these mythical stories are distributed as reading matter through the fourth and fifth grades. They constitute a large share of the most famous literature of the great civilized nations. It is worth while to name over the virtues of these stories and poems.

They have sprung directly out of the people's life, they are race products, worked over from age to age by poetic spirits, and finally gathered into enduring form by a Homer, Virgil, or Spenser. The best of our later poets and prose masters have employed their finest skill in rendering them into simple and poetic English, as Bryant, Kingsley, Longfellow, Pope, Hawthorne, Palmer, Tennyson, Church, and many more.

They are the best descriptions we have of the customs, ideas, and dress, the homes, habits, and motives, of the ancestral races. Many other sources, as temples, ruins, tombs, coins, etc., help to explain this early history; but this literature calls it again into life and puts meaning into all other sources of knowledge.

The influence which this early literature has had upon later historical growth of the great races is overwhelming, and is plain to the eyes of even unscholarly persons. The root from which the marvellous tree of Greek civilization grew is seen in Homer's poems.

In these myths we find those commanding characters which typify the strength and virtues of the race, as Achilles, Ulysses, Siegfried, Penelope, Thor, Apollo, Theseus, Hiawatha, Orpheus, Diana, Vulcan, Prometheus, and the Muses.

A close acquaintance with these creative ideas of the early world is necessary to an understanding of all subsequent life and literature. And it is not merely the names of Greek divinities and definitions of their character and qualities which put meaning into the numberless allusions of modern writers. One reason why many modern thinkers smile at the triteness and childishness of Greek fable is, that they have not caught the spirit and meaning of the Greek story. The great masters of thought, like Goethe, Shakespeare, Emerson, Tennyson, and Bryant, have seen deeper.

It is, moreover, in childhood, during the early school years especially, that we may best appreciate and enjoy these poetic creations of an early world. It is hardly to be expected that people whose youth has been clamped into the mould of commonplace and sensuous facts, and whose later years have been crusted over with modern materialism and commercialism, should listen with any patience to Orpheus and the Muses, or even to the wood notes of Pan.

We hardly need to dwell upon the idea that the old heroic myths are the delight of boys and girls, and that this sympathy for the myth is the foundation of its educative power. Nor is it the purpose of the school to warp the minds of children into this one channel of growth. The historical and scientific studies run parallel with the myth, and give strength for realities.

It is not difficult to see that music, the drama, and the fine arts spring from these old myths as from their chief source. They furnish motive to many of the greatest works of dramatist, composer, painter, and sculptor, in all the ages since. Æschylus and the Greek dramatists, Goethe and Wagner, Fénelon and Shakespeare, drew abundantly from these sources.

A few of the striking characters of this great age of heroic myths should be treated with such fulness as to stand out clearly to the children and appeal to the heart as well as to the head. Ulysses and Siegfried stand in the centre of two of the chief stories, and exemplify great qualities of character, strength, wisdom, and nobleness of mind.

In the third grade the children have had an oral introduction to some of the old stories, and have had a spirited entrance to Mythland. This oral treatment of the stories is a fitting and necessary prelude to the reading work of the fourth and fifth grades. It is more fully discussed, together with the art of the story-teller, in "The Special Method in Primary Reading and Story."

Closely related to the myths, and kindred in spirit, are such choice reading materials as "The Arabian Nights," "King of the Golden River," Stockton's "Fanciful Tales," "The Pied Piper," and a number of shorter poems and stories found in the collections recommended for fourth and fifth grades. Some of Hawthorne's and Irving's stories belong also to this group.

2. Ballads and Traditional Stories.

A somewhat distinct group of the best reading for fourth and fifth grades is found in the historical ballads and national legends from the early history of England, Germany, Italy, and France. They include such selections as "Sir Patrick Spens," "The Ballads of Robin Hood," "Horatius," "Bannockburn," "The Heart of the Bruce," "The Story of Regulus," of "Cincinnatus," "Alfred the Harper," and many more. In the list of books recommended for children's reading are several ballad books, Macaulay's "Lays of Ancient Rome," "The Book of Golden Deeds," "Tales from English History," and several others, with great variety of poem and story. Many of these selections are short and spirited and well suited to awaken the strongest enthusiasm of children. They are sometimes in dialogue form, both in prose and verse, have strong dramatic action, and are thus helpful in variety and force of expression. There is also much early history and national spirit involved. The old historical ballads and traditions have great educative value. They are simple, crude, and powerful, and awaken the spirit to receive the message of heroism. In her introduction to the "Ballad Book," Katharine Lee Bates says, "For these primitive folk-songs, which have done so much to educate the poetic sense in the fine peasantry of Scotland—that peasantry which has produced an Ayreshire Ploughman and an Ettric Shepherd—are assuredly,

"'Thanks to the human heart by which it lives,'

among the best educators that can be brought into our schoolrooms."

"The Lays of Ancient Rome," the "Ballads," and the "Tales from English History" belong to the heroic series. Though far separated in time and place, they breathe the same spirit of personal energy, self-sacrifice, and love of country. They reveal manly resistance to cruelty and tyranny. We may begin this series with a term's work upon Macaulay's "Lays" and a few other choice stories in prose and verse. Thereafter we may insert other ballads, where needed, in connection with history, and in amplification of longer stories or masterpieces like Scott's "Tales of a Grandfather," and "Marmion." In the fifth grade, children are of an age when these stories of heroism in olden days strike a responsive chord. They delight in such tales, memorize them, and enter into the full energy of their spirited reproduction.

The main purpose at first is to appreciate their thought as an expression of history, tradition, and national life. A complete and absorbing study of a single series of these ballads, as of Macaulay's, supplies also an excellent standard of comparison for other more or less similar episodes in the history of Switzerland, Greece, England, and America.

These historical legends merge almost imperceptibly into the historical tales of early English, Roman, and French or German history. The patriarchal stories of the Old Testament furnish the finest of early history stories and should be included in these materials. "The Old Stories of the East," and "Old Testament Stories in Scripture Language" are among the best.

3. Stories of Chivalry.

Tales of chivalry, beginning with "Arthur and his Round Table Knights," "Roland and Oliver," and other mediæval tales, have a great attraction for poets and children. Such books are included in our lists as "The Court of King Arthur," the "Story of Roland," "Tales of Chivalry," "The Boys' King Arthur," the "Age of Chivalry," and "The Coming of Arthur" and "Passing of Arthur." There are also many shorter poems touching this spirit of chivalry in the Ballad literature. The character and spirit of King Arthur as revealed in the matchless music of Tennyson should find its way to the hearts of children before they leave the school. Like Sir Galahad, he could say,

> "My strength is as the strength of ten
> Because my heart is pure."

4. Historical Stories and Poems.

In the fifth and sixth grades children should begin to read some of the best biographical and historical stories of America and of European countries. Of these we have excellent materials from many lands and periods of time, such as Higginson's "American Explorers," Morris's "Historical Tales" (both American and English), "Stories of American Life and Adventure," "Stories of Our Country," "Pioneer History Stories," "Ten Boys on the Road from Long Ago," "The Story of the English," "Stories from Herodotus," "Pilgrims and Puritans," Hawthorne's "Biographical Stories," "Stories from American Life," and others.

In the oral history lessons given on alternate days in fourth grade (see special method in history) we have made a spirited entrance to American history through the pioneer stories of the Mississippi Valley. These should precede and pave the way for classic readings in American history. In the fifth grade, the stories of Columbus and of the chief navigators, also the narratives of the Atlantic coast pioneers, are told. The regular history work of the sixth grade should be a study of the growth of the leading colonies during the colonial period and the French and Indian Wars.

In the fifth grade we may begin to read some of the hero narratives of our own pioneer epoch as rendered by the best writers; for instance, Higginson's "American Explorers," "Pilgrims and Puritans," "Stories of Our Country," and "Grandfather's Chair." They are lifelike and spirited, and introduce us to the realism of our early history in its rugged exposure and trials, while they bring out those stern but high ideals of life which the Puritan and the Cavalier, the navigator, the pioneer hunter, and explorer illustrate. Higginson's collection of letters and reports of the early explorers, with their quaint language and eye-witness descriptions, is strikingly vivid in its portraiture of early scenes upon our shores. Hawthorne, in "Grandfather's Chair," has moulded the hardy biography of New England leaders into literary form.

5. Great Biographies.

In addition to the shorter biographical stories just mentioned, as children advance into the sixth, seventh, and eighth grades, they should make a close acquaintance with a few of the great biographies. There is an abundance of excellent American biographies, but we should limit ourselves to those most important and best suited to influence the character of young people. It is necessary also to use those which have been written in a style easily comprehended by the children. Some of the best are as follows: Scudder's "Life of Washington," Franklin's "Autobiography," Hosmer's "Life of Samuel Adams," and the lives of John Quincy Adams, Daniel Webster, and Lincoln in the "Statesman Series." There are two fairly good books of

Lincoln's early life for children. There are also many shorter biographies included in the books recommended for regular or collateral reading.

In style and content the story of Franklin is one of the best for children. The "Autobiography" of Franklin has many graphic touches from American life. His intense practical personality, his many-sidedness and public spirit, make up a character that will long instruct and open out in many directions the minds of the young. His clear sense and wisdom in small affairs as in great, and the pleasing style of his narrative, are sufficiently characteristic to have a strong personal impression. It will hardly be necessary to take the whole of the "Autobiography," but the more attractive parts, leaving the rest to the private reading of children. "Poor Richard's Almanac" intensifies the notion of Franklin's practical and everyday wisdom, and at the same time introduces the children to a form of literature that, in colonial days, under Franklin's patronage, had a wide acceptance and lasting influence in America.

Plutarch's "Lives" furnish a series of great biographies which grammar school children should become well acquainted with. The lives of American writers and poets should be brought to the attention of children in conjunction with their productions. "The Children's Stories of American Literature" and the introductory chapters of many of the masterpieces furnish this interesting and stimulating material. It should not be neglected by pupils and teachers. For older pupils and for teachers several of Macaulay's "Essays" are valuable, and the style is strikingly interesting. For example, the essays on Samuel Johnson, Lord Chatham, Milton, Addison, and Frederick the Great. Motley's "Essay on Peter the Great" and Carlyle's "Essay on Burns" are of similar interest and value. "The Schönberg Cotta Family" is valuable in the upper grammar grades. Most of this kind of reading must be outside reference work if it is done at all. Teachers should, first of all, enrich their own experience by these readings, occasionally bring a book to the class from which selections may be read, and, secondly, encourage the more enthusiastic and capable children to this wider field of reading.

6. Historical Poems and Pictures of American Life.

Some of the best American poems and prose masterpieces are fine descriptions of American life and manners, in different parts of the country and at various times. Such are: "Courtship of Miles Standish," "Tales of the White Hills," "Snow-Bound," "Rip Van Winkle," and "Sleepy Hollow." "The Gentle Boy," "Mabel Martin," "Giles Corey," "Evangeline," "Uncle Tom's Cabin," and some of the great biographies, like those of Samuel Adams, Franklin, Washington, and Lincoln, are also fine descriptions of home life in America. The same may be said of some of the masterpieces of English and European literature, for example, "Ivanhoe," "Roger de Coverley," "The Christmas Carol," "Vicar of Wakefield," "William Tell," "Silas Marner," "The Cotter's Saturday Night," and "Schönberg Cotta Family."

The culture value of these pictures of home and domestic life for young people is surpassingly great. Gradually their views are broadened, and they may be imbued with those social, home-bred qualities and virtues so fundamental in human life.

Irving's stories and Longfellow's "Miles Standish" give a still more pronounced and pleasing literary cast to two of the characteristic forms of life in our colonial history, the Puritan and the Dutch Patroon. If the children have reached this point, where they can read and enjoy the "Sketch-Book," it will be worth much as a description of life along the Hudson, and will develop taste and appreciation for literary excellence. Even the fanciful and ridiculous elements conduce to mental health and soundness, by showing up in pleasing satire the weaknesses and foibles of well-meaning people.

"Snow-Bound," "Songs of Labor," and "Among the Hills," while not historical in the usual sense, are still plainly American, and may well be associated with other poetic delineations of American life. "Snow-Bound" is a picture of New England life, with its pleasing and deep-rooted memories. Its family spirit and idealization of common objects and joys make it a classic which reaches the hearts of boys and girls. "Among the Hills" is also a picture of home life in New England mountains, a contrast of the mean and low in home environment to the beauty of thrift and taste and unselfish home joys. The "Songs of Labor" are descriptive of the toils and spirit of our varied employments in New England and of that larger

New England which the migrating Yankees have established between the oceans.

"Evangeline" is another literary pearl that enshrines in sad and mournful measures a story of colonial days, and teaches several great lessons, as of the harshness and injustice of war, of fair-mindedness and sympathy for those of alien speech and country, of patience and gentleness and loyalty to high ideals in a character familiar and sacred to all.

7. The Poetry of Nature in the Masterpieces of Literature.

Both in poetic and in prose form there is great variety and depth of nature worship in good literature. There are few, if any, of the great poets who have not been enthusiastic and sympathetic observers of nature,—nature lovers, we may call them. We can hardly mention the names of Emerson, Bryant, and Wordsworth, without thinking of their loving companionship with nature, their flight to the woods and fields. But the same is true of Lowell, Whittier, Hawthorne, Whitman, and all the rest. When we add to these, those companions of nature, such as Thoreau, Leander Keyser, Olive Thorn Miller, Burroughs, Warner, and others of like spirit, we may be surprised at the number of our leading writers who have found their chief delight in dwelling close to the heart of nature.

An examination of the books recommended for children's study and delight will reveal a large number of the most graceful, inspiring products of human thought, which are nature poems, nature hymns, odes to skylark, the dandelion, the mountain daisy, communings with the myriad moods and forms of the natural world. Such books as "Nature Pictures by American Poets," "Golden Treasury of Songs and Lyrics," "Poetry of the Seasons," the "Open Sesame" books, and others, show an infinite variety of poetic inspiration from nature. Adding to these Burroughs's "Birds and Bees," "Wake Robin," "Squirrels and other Fur-bearers"; Thoreau's "Succession of Forest Trees"; Higginson's "Outdoor Papers"; Keyser's "News from the Birds," "In Bird Land," and "Birddom"; Torrey's "Footpath Way," and "Birds in the Bush"; Long's "Wilderness Ways," and "Ways of Wood Folk"; the "Plant World" of Vincent, the "Natural History" of Selborne, and others of like quality,—and we have an abundance of the most friendly and enticing invitations to nature study. These materials are suited, by proper arrangement, to all the grades from the fourth up. Under good teachers such books can do no other than awaken and encourage the happiest kind of observation and sympathy for nature. It is the kind of appreciation of birds and trees, insects and clouds, which at once trains to close and discriminating perception, and to the cultivation of æsthetic sense in color, form, and sound.

The love of nature cannot be better instilled than by following these poets.

While the study of literature as it images nature cannot take the place of pure science, it is the most powerful ally that the scientist can call in. The poets can do as much to idealize science study, to wake the dull eye, and quicken the languid interest in nature, as scientists themselves. Away, then, with this presumed antagonism between literature and science! Neither is complete without the other. Neither can stand on its own feet. But together, in mutual support, they cannot be tripped up. The facts, the laws, the utilities, adaptations, and wonders in nature are not so marvellous but the poet's eye will pierce beneath and above them, will give them a deeper interpretation, and clothe them in a garment of beauty and praise. There is nothing beautiful or grand or praiseworthy that the poet's eye will not detect it, and the poet's art reveal it in living and lasting forms. Let the scientist delve and the poet sing. The messages between them should be only those of cheer.

It is in this myriad-voiced world of fields and brooks, of mountain, lake, and river, of storm and cloud and of the changing seasons, that poets find the images, suggestions, and analogies which interpret and illustrate the spiritual life of man. The more rigid study of science in laboratory and class-room is necessary to the student, but it would be a narrow and pedantic teacher who would not welcome the poetic temper and enthusiasm in nature study.

The teachers of reading have, therefore, the best of all opportunities for cultivating this many-sided sympathy for and insight into nature, and at the same time to train the children to correlate these nature poems with their science studies. Observers like Thoreau and Burroughs give us the greatest inducement for getting out into the woods. They open our eyes to the beauties and our hearts to the truth of nature's teachings. These are the gardens of delight where science and poetry walk hand in hand and speak face to face. It would not be difficult to show that many of the greatest scientists were poets, and that some of the chiefest poets have been foremost in scientific study.

8. The Sentiment of Patriotism in Literature.

The powerful national spirit finds expression in many forms of literature, in hymns, in war song, in oration, in essay, in pioneer narrative, in stories of battle, in novel, in flag song, in ballad, and in biography.

We have already noted the great significance of American history stories in fourth and fifth grades. It is from the early pioneer epoch and the colonial history that we derive much of our best educative history. The heroism of these old days has been commemorated in story and poem by our best writers.

As we approach the Revolutionary crisis a new body of choice literary products, aglow with the fire of patriotism and independence, is found stored up for the joy and stimulus of our growing young Americans: "Paul Revere's Ride," "Grandmother's Story of Bunker Hill," Washington's letters, "A Ballad of the Boston Tea Party," "Ode for Washington's Birthday," "Lexington" (Holmes), "The Song of Marion's Men," "The Green Mountain Boys," Webster's speeches at Bunker Hill and on Adams and Jefferson, "Old Ticonderoga" (Hawthorne), Burke's speech on the American War, Washington's "Farewell to the Army," The Declaration of Independence, "Under the Old Elm," and descriptions of some of the great scenes of the war by our best historians.

It is to be desired that children in the seventh grade may have opportunity in regular history lessons to study in detail a few of the central topics of the Revolutionary epoch. This will put them in touch with the spirit and surroundings of the Americans.

In the reading lessons of the same grade we may well afford to discover and feel what our best patriots and men of letters have said and felt in view of the struggle for freedom. The noblest expressions of sentiment upon great men and their achievements are contagious with the young. Patriotism can find no better soil in which to strike its deepest roots than the noble outbursts of our orators and poets and patriotic statesmen. The cumulative effect of these varied but kindred materials is greater than when scattered and disconnected. They mutually support each other, and when they are brought into close dependence upon parallel historical studies, we may well say that the children are drinking from the deep and pure sources of true Americanism.

Parallel to whatever history we attempt to teach in the eighth grade should run a selection of the best literary products that our American authors can furnish, and here again we are rich in resources. The thought and life of our people find their high-water mark in the poet's clarion note and the statesman's impassioned appeal. No others have perceived the destiny of our young republic as our cherished poets, Longfellow, Whittier, Bryant, Holmes, and Emerson. They have stood upon the mountain tops, looking far and wide through the clear atmosphere, while the great army of the people has been tenting in the valleys below. These wakeful priests and prophets have caught the bright tints of the morning while the people were still asleep, and have witnessed the suffused glory of the sunset clouds when the weary masses below had already forgotten the day's toil. One thing at least, and that the greatest, can be done for our children before they finish the common school course. They may rise into this pure atmosphere of poet, patriot, sage, and prophet. They may hear these deathless strains and feel the thrill of these clarion notes. Let their ears be once attuned to the strength and harmony of this music, and it will not cease to echo in their deeper life. The future patriots will be at hand, and the coming years will see them rising to the great duties that inevitably await them. We have a body of noble, patriotic material which is capable of producing this effect if handled by skilful teachers: the Ordinance of 1787, *The Federalist*, Numbers 1 and 2, Washington's "Inaugurals" and the "Farewell Address," Everett's "Oration on Washington," "O Mother of Mighty Race" (Bryant); "Our Country's Call" (Bryant); "Abraham Lincoln" (Bryant); Lincoln's "Inaugurals" and "Gettysburg Speech," "Army Hymn" and "The Flower of Liberty" (Holmes), Webster's "Second Speech on Foot's Resolution," The Emancipation Proclamation, "The Fortune of the Republic" (Emerson), etc., "Antiquity of Freedom" (Bryant); "Centennial Hymn" (Whittier); "The

Building of the Ship" (Longfellow); "The Poor Voter on Election Day" (Whittier).

Why not gather together these sources of power, of unselfish patriotism, of self-sacrifice, of noble and inspiring impulse? Let this fruit-bringing seed be sown deep in the minds and hearts of the receptive young. What has inspired the best of men to high thinking and living can touch them.

It is not by reading and declaiming a few miscellaneous fragments of patriotic gush, not by waving flags and banners and following processions, that the deeper sentiments of patriotism and humanity are to be touched, but by gathering and concentrating these fuller, richer sources of spiritual power and conscious national destiny. The schoolroom is by far the best place to consolidate these purifying and conserving sentiments. By gathering into a rising series and focussing in the higher grades the various forms, in prose and verse, in which the genius of our country has found its strongest expression; by associating these ringing sentiments with the epochs and crises of our history, with the valorous deeds of patriots upon the field and of statesmen in the senate, with the life and longings of home-nurtured poets and sages,—we shall plant seed whose fruitage will not disappoint the lovers of the fatherland.

Mr. Horace E. Scudder, in his two essays on "Literature" and "American Classics in the Common School," has portrayed with convincing clearness the spiritual power and high-toned Americanism which breathe from those literary monuments which have been quarried from our own hillsides and chiselled by American hands. We recommend to every teacher the reading in full of these essays, from which we quote at much length:—

"Fifty years ago there were living in America six men of mark, of whom the youngest was then nineteen years of age, the oldest forty-four. Three of the six are in their graves and three still breathe the kindly air. [Since this was written, in 1888, the last of the six has passed away.] One only of the six has held high place in the national councils, and it is not by that distinction that he is known and loved. They have not been in battle; they have had no armies at their command; they have not amassed great fortunes, nor have great industries waited on their movements. Those pageants of circumstances which kindle the imagination have been remote from their names. They were born on American soil; they have breathed American air; they were nurtured on American ideas. They are Americans of Americans. They are as truly the issue of our national life as are the common schools in which we glory. During the fifty years in which our common school system has been growing up to maturity these six have lived and sung; and I dare say that the lives and songs of Bryant, Emerson, Longfellow, Whittier, Holmes, and Lowell have an imperishable value, regarded as exponents of national life, not for a moment to be outweighed in the balance by the most elaborate system of common schools which the wit of man may devise. The nation may command armies and schools to rise from the soil, but it cannot call into life a poet. Yet when the poet comes and we hear his voice in the upper air, then we know the nation he owns is worthy of the name. Do men gather grapes of thorns or figs of thistles? Even so, pure poetry springs from no rank soil of national life.

"I am not arguing for the critical study of our great authors, in the higher grades of our schools. They are not the best subjects for critical scholarship; criticism demands greater remoteness, greater foreignness of nature. Moreover, critical study is not the surest method of securing the full measure of spiritual light, though it yields abundant gain in the refinement of the intellectual nature and in the quickening of the perceptive faculties. I am arguing for the free, generous use of these authors in the principal years of school life. It is then that their power is most profoundly needed, and will be most strongly felt. We need to put our children in their impressionable years into instant and close connection with the highest manifestation of our national life. Away with the bottle and the tube! Give them a lusty draft at the mother's full breast!

"Nor do I fear that such a course will breed a narrow and parochial Americanism. On the contrary, it would destroy a vulgar pride in country, help the young to see humanity from the heights on which the masters of song have dwelt, and open the mind to the more hospitable entertainment of the best literature of every clime and age. I am convinced that there is no surer way to introduce the best English literature into our schools than to give the place of honor to American literature. In the order of nature a youth must be a citizen of his own country before he can become naturalized in the world. We recognize this in our geography and history; we may wisely recognize it also in our reading.

"The place, then, of literature in our common school education is in spiritualizing life, letting light into the mind, inspiring and feeding the higher forces of human nature.

"It is the business of the old to transmit to the young the great traditions of the past of the country, to feed anew the undying flame of patriotism. There is the element of destiny. No nation lives upon its past; it is already dead when it says, 'Let us eat and drink to-day; for to-morrow we die.' But what that destiny is to be may be read in the ideals which the young are forming; and those ideals, again, it is the business of the old to guide. They cannot form them; the young must form them for themselves; but whether these ideals shall be large or petty, honorable or mean, will depend upon the sustenance on which they are fed.

"Now in a democracy, more signally than under any other form of national organization, it is vitally necessary that there should be an unceasing, unimpeded circulation of the spiritual life of the people. The sacrifice of the men and women who have made and preserved America, from the days of Virginia and New England to this hour, has been ascending from the earth in a never-ending cloud; they have fallen again in strains of music, in sculpture, in painting, in memorial hall, in tale, in oration, in poem, in consecration of life; and the spirit which ascended is the same as that which descended. In literature above all is this spirit enshrined. You have but to throw open the shrine, and the spirit comes with its outspread blessings upon millions of waiting souls. Entering them, it reissues in countless shapes, and thus is the life of the nation in its highest form kept ever in motion, and without motion is no life.

"The deposit of nationality is in laws, institutions, art, character, and religion; but laws, institutions, character, and religion are expressed through art and mainly through the art of letters. It is literature, therefore, that holds in precipitation the genius of the country; and the higher the form of literature, the more consummate the expression of that spirit which does not so much seek a materialization as it shapes itself inevitably in fitting form. Long may we read and ponder the life of Washington, yet at last fall back content upon those graphic lines of Lowell in 'Under the Old Elm,' which cause the figure of the great American to outline itself upon the imagination with large and strong portraiture. The spirit of the orations of Webster and

Benton, the whole history of the young giant poised in conscious strength before his triumphant struggle, one may catch in a breath in those glowing lines which end 'The Building of the Ship.' The deep passion of the war for the Union may be overlooked in some formal study of battles and campaigns, but rises pure, strong, and flaming in the immortal 'Gettysburg Speech.'

"Precisely thus the sentiment of patriotism must be kept fresh and living in the hearts of the young through quick and immediate contact with the sources of that sentiment; and the most helpful means are those spiritual deposits of patriotism which we find in noble poetry and lofty prose, as communicated by men who have lived patriotic lives and been fed with coals from the altar.

"It is from the men and women bred on American soil that the fittest words come for the spiritual enrichment of American youth. I believe heartily in the advantage of enlarging one's horizon by taking in other climes and other ages, but first let us make sure of that great expansive power which lies close at hand. I am sure there never was a time or country where national education, under the guidance of national art and thought, was so possible as in America to-day.

"The body of wholesome, strong American literature is large enough to make it possible to keep boys and girls upon it from the time when they begin to recognize the element of authorship until they leave the school, and it is varied and flexible enough to give employment to the mind in all its stages of development. Moreover, this literature is interesting, and is allied with interesting concerns; half the hard places are overcome by the willing mind, and the boy who stumbles over some jejune lesson in his reading-book will run over a bit of genuine prose from Irving which the schoolbook maker, with his calipers, pronounces too hard.

"We have gone quite far enough in the mechanical development of the common school system. What we most need is the breath of life, and reading offers the noblest means for receiving and imparting this breath of life. The spiritual element in education in our common schools will be found to lie in reserve in literature, and, as I believe, most effectively in American literature.

"Think for a moment of that great, silent, resistless power for good which might at this moment be lifting the youth of the country, were the hours for reading in school expended upon the undying, life-giving books! Think of the substantial growth of a generous Americanism, were the boys and girls to be fed from the fresh springs of American literature! It would be no narrow provincialism into which they would emerge. The windows in Longfellow's mind looked to the east, and the children who have entered into possession of his wealth travel far. Bryant's flight carries one through upper air, over broad champaigns. The lover of Emerson has learned to get a remote vision. The companion of Thoreau finds Concord become suddenly the centre of a very wide horizon. Irving has annexed Spain to America. Hawthorne has nationalized the gods of Greece and given an atmosphere to New England. Whittier has translated the Hebrew Scriptures into the American dialect. Lowell gives the American boy an academy without cutting down a stick of timber in the grove, or disturbing the birds. Holmes supplies that hickory which makes one careless of the crackling of thorns. Franklin makes the America of a past generation a part of the great world before treaties had bound the floating states into formal connection with venerable nations. What is all this but saying that the rich inheritance we have is no local ten-acre lot, but a part of the undivided estate of humanity. Universality, Cosmopolitanism,—these are fine words, but no man ever secured the freedom of the Universe who did not first pay taxes and vote in his own village."—"Literature in School" (Houghton, Mifflin, & Co.).

9. The series of American classics is nowise confined to the ideas of local or national patriotism, but above and beyond that deep and powerful sentiment which magnifies the opportunity and manifest destiny of our nation, it grasps at the ideal form and content of those Christian virtues which now and evermore carry healing and comfort to the toiling millions. Our poets, as they have pondered on the past and looked into the future, were not able to be content with less than the best. As the vision of the coming years unrolled itself before them they looked upon it with joy mingled with solicitude. In the mighty conflicts now upon us only those of generous and saintly purpose and of pure hearts can prevail.

> "Brief is the time, I know,
> The warfare scarce begun;
> Yet all may win the triumphs thou hast won.
> Still flows the fount whose waters strengthened thee,
> The victors' names are yet too few to fill
> Heaven's mighty roll; the glorious armory
> That ministered to thee is open still."—BRYANT.

To reveal this Christian armory, the defences of the soul against the assaults of evil, has been the highest inspiration of our poets. What depth and beauty and impersonation of Christian virtues do we find in "Snow-Bound," "Among the Hills," "Evangeline," "The Conqueror's Grave," "To a Waterfowl," "The Groves were God's First Temples," "The Living Temple," "The Sun Day Hymn," "The Chambered Nautilus," "Vision of Sir Launfal," "The Great Stone Face."

The Bible is not generally admissible as a schoolbook, but the spirit of Christianity, clad in the forms of strength and grace, is immanent in the works of our poets. So universal, so human, so fit to the needs and destinies of men, are the truths of the great evangel, that the prophets and seers of our race drift evermore into the sheltering haven they supply. To drink in these potent truths through poetry and song, to see them enshrined in the imagery and fervor of the sacred masterpieces of our literature, is more than culture, more than morality; it is the portal and sanctuary of religious thought, and children may enter it.

10. The higher products of literature contain an energy that quickens spiritual life in morals, in art, and in religion. To many people, whose lives are submerged in commercial pursuits or in the great struggle to develop and utilize the material resources of the world, these spiritual forces seem vague and shadowy, if not mythical. But there are plenty of heroic souls in the realm of letters, such as Emerson, Scudder, Ruskin, Arnold, and Carlyle, who are not disposed to let men settle down in lazy satisfaction with material good, nor to be blinded even by the splendor of modern achievements in engineering, in medicine, and in the application of electricity. We must at least reach a point of view high enough to perceive the relations of these natural riches to the higher nature and destiny of man.

Scudder says, "It is to literature that we must look for the substantial protection of the growing mind against an ignoble, material conception of life, and for the inspiring power which shall lift the nature into its rightful fellowship with whatsoever is noble, true, lovely, and of good report."

Shelley, in like spirit, says: "The cultivation of poetry is never more to be desired than at periods when, from an excess of the selfish and calculating principle, the accumulation of the materials of external life exceed the quantity of the power of assimilating them to the internal laws of human nature. The body has then become too unwieldy for that which animates it."

Matthew Arnold, in "Sweetness and Light," while discussing the function of that truer culture and "perfection which consists in becoming something rather than in having something," remarks:—

"And this function is particularly important in our modern world, of which the whole civilization is, to a much greater degree than the civilization of Greece and Rome, mechanical and external, and tends constantly to become more so. But above all in our own country has culture a weighty part to perform because here that mechanical character, which civilization tends to take everywhere, is shown in the most eminent degree. Indeed, nearly all the characters of perfection, as culture teaches us to fix them, meet in this country with some powerful tendency which thwarts them and sets them at defiance. The idea of perfection as an inward condition of the mind and spirit is at variance with the mechanical and material civilization in esteem with us, and nowhere, as I have said, so much in esteem as with us."

11. Judged by these higher standards our writers and literary leaders were not simply Americans. They were also Europeans. The Puritan brought his religion with him, the Cavalier acquired his gentlemanly instincts in the old home, not in the untrodden forests of the New World. Much of what we call American is the wine of the Old World poured into the bearskins and buckskins of the West, with a flavor of the freedom of our Western wilds. Though born and bred on American soil and to the last exemplars of the American spirit, our literary leaders have derived their ideas and inspiration from the literature, tradition, and history of the Old World. It will be no small part of our purpose, therefore, to open up to the children of our

common schools the best entrance to the history and literature of Europe. Our own writers and poets have done this for us in a variety of instances: Hawthorne's rendering of the Greek myths, Bryant's translation of the "Iliad" and "Odyssey," a good half of Irving's "Sketch-Book," Lowell's "Vision of Sir Launfal," "Aladdin," and "Prometheus," Irving's "Alhambra," Longfellow's "Golden Legend," "Sandalphon," Taylor's "Boys of Other Countries." Nearly the whole of our literature, even when dealing ostensibly with American topics, is suffused with the spirit and imagery of the Old World traditions. There is also a large collection of prose versions of European traditions, which, while not classic, are still lively renderings of old stories and well suited to the collateral reading of children. Such are "Gods and Heroes," "Tales from English History," "Tales from Spenser," "Heroes of Asgard," "Story of the Iliad and Odyssey."

The transition from our own poets who have handled European themes to English writers who have done the same, is easy and natural; Macaulay's "Lays of Ancient Rome," Scott's "Tales of a Grandfather," "The Stories of Waverley," the "Christmas Carol," Kingsley's "Greek Heroes" and "Water Babies," Ruskin's "King of the Golden River," "Lady of the Lake," "Marmion," "Roger de Coverley Papers," "Merchant of Venice," "Arabian Nights," "Peasant and Prince," Bunyan's "Pilgrim's Progress," "Gulliver's Travels," and others have become by inheritance and birthright as much a part of the American child's culture as the more distinctive products of our own writers. No line can be drawn between those writings which are American and those which sprung from the soil of England and Europe. So intimate and vital is the connection between our present and our past, between our children and their cousins across the water.

These American and European literary products lie side by side in the school course, though the predominating spirit through the middle and higher grades up to the eighth should be American. We have noticed that in the earlier grades most of our classic reading matter comes from Europe, the nursery rhymes, the folk-lore, fables, and myths, because the childhood of our culture periods was in Europe. But into the fourth grade, and from there on, beginning with the pioneers on sea and land, our American history and literature enters as a powerful agent of culture. It brings us into quick and vital contact, not simply with the outward facts, but with the inmost spirit, of our national life and struggle toward development. This gives the

American impulse free and full expansion, and fortunate are we, beyond expression, that pure and lofty poets stand at the threshold to usher the children into this realm, founded deep in the realism of our past history and rising grandly into the idealism of our desires and hopes. As we advance into the sixth, seventh, and eighth grades the literature of Europe begins again to increase in quantity and influence, and to share equally with American authors the attention of the children.

The Americanism of our poets and prose writers, as previously shown, has also another side to it, which is one sign of the breadth and many-sidedness of literature as a study for the young. North America is a land rich in variety of natural scenery and resource. Nature has decked the New World with a lavish hand, forest and mountain, lake and river, prairie and desert, the summer land of flowers and the home of New England winters. The masterpieces of our poets are full of the scenery, vegetation, sunsets, mountains, and prairies of the Western empire. The flowers, the birds, the wild beasts, the pathless forests, the limitless stretches of plain, have mirrored themselves in the songs of our poets, and have rendered them dearer to us because seen and realized in this idealism. Unconsciously perhaps the feeling of patriotism is largely based upon this knowledge of the rich and varied beauty and bounty of our native land.

> "I love thy rocks and rills,
> Thy woods and templed hills,
> My heart with rapture thrills,
>   Like that above."

As along the shores of our Northern lakes the clear and quiet waters reflect the green banks, the rolling, forest-crowned hills, the rocky bluffs, the floating clouds, and overarching blue, so in the homespun, classic verse and prose of our own writers are imaged the myriad charms of our native land. Bryant especially is the poet of forest and glade, "The Forest Hymn," "The Death of the Flowers," "The Return of the Birds," "A Summer Ramble," "The Fringed Gentian," "The Hunter of the Prairies," "The White-footed Deer," "To a Waterfowl," "Thanatopsis," and many others. Longfellow's "Hiawatha," "Evangeline"; Whittier's "Barefoot Boy," "Songs of Labor," "Among the Hills," and "Snow-Bound"; Hawthorne's "Tales of the White Hills"; Holmes's "Spring"; Lowell's "Indian Summer Reverie," "The Oak," and many more.

The literature selected for these grades has a wide scope. It is instinct with the best Americanism. It draws from Europe at every breath, while enjoying the freedom of the West. Social, political, and home life and virtue are portrayed in great variety of dress. Nature also and natural science reveal the myriad forms of beauty and utility.

CHAPTER IV

CLASS-ROOM METHOD IN READING

1. The Doorway.

There is a strong comfort in the idea that in the preparation of a masterpiece for a reading class the teacher may be dealing with a unity of thought in a variety of relations that makes the study a comprehensive culture-product both to herself and to the children. To become a student of "Hiawatha" as a whole, and in its relations to Indian life and tradition, early aboriginal history, and Longfellow's connection with the same, is to throw a deep glance into history and anthropology, and to recognize literature as the permanent form of expressing their spirit. There are a good many sidelights that a teacher needs to get from history and other literature, and from the author's life, in order to see a literary masterpiece in its true setting. It is the part of the poet to make his work intensely real and ideal, the two elements that appeal with trenchant force to children. The teacher needs not only to see the graphic pictures drawn by the artist, but to gather about these central points of view other collateral, explanatory facts that give a deeper setting to the picture. Fortunately, such study as this is not burdensome. There is a joyousness and sparkle to it that can relieve many an hour of tedium. Literature in its best forms is recreation, and brings an infusion of spiritual energy. We should not allow ourselves to confuse it with those more humdrum forms of school employment, like spelling, figuring, reading in the formal sense, grammar, writing, etc. Literature is the spiritual side of school effort, the uplands of thought, where gushing springs well from the roots and shade of overarching trees. There is jollity and music, beauty and grandeur, the freshness of cool breezes and of mountain scenery, in such profusion as to satisfy the exuberance of youthful spirit, and to infuse new energy into old and tired natures. If the teacher can only get out of the narrow streets of the town and from between the dead walls of the schoolroom, up among the meadows and groves and brooks, in company with Bryant or Longfellow or Whittier, if she can only take a draught of these spirit-waters before walking into the schoolroom, her thought and conduct will be tempered into a fit instrument of culture.

The teacher's preparation is not only in the intellectual grasp of the thought, but in the sympathy, feeling, and pleasure germane to a classic. The æsthetic and emotional elements, the charm of poetry, and the sparkle of wit and glint of literary elegance and aptness are what give relish and delight to true literary products. Literature appeals to the whole nature and not to the intellect alone. It is not superficial and formal, but deep and spiritual. The teacher who reads a classic like "Marmion," thoughtfully dwelling upon the historic pictures, calling to mind other of Scott's stories and the earlier struggle between Scotland and England, is drinking at the fresh fountains and sources of some of the best parts of European history. The clear and rock-rimmed lakes of Scotland, her rugged mountains and ruined castle walls, are not more delightful to the traveller than the pictures of life and history that appear in "Tales of a Grandfather," "Rob Roy," "Marmion," and "Lady of the Lake." To paint these stirring panoramic views of Scotch adventure and prowess upon the imagination of the young is to invigorate their thought with the real sentiment of patriotism, and with appreciation for manly struggle, endurance, and spirit. The vivid insight it gives into feudal society in church and court and castle, on battle-field and in dining hall, among the rude peasantry and the unlettered nobility, is found more lifelike and lasting than the usual results of historical study.

The moment we take a longer masterpiece and examine it as a representative piece of human life, or as a typical portraiture of a historical epoch, it becomes the converging point for much lively and suggestive knowledge, deep and strong social interests, and convincing personification of moral impulses.

The best preparation, therefore, a teacher can make for a class is a spiritual and spirited one. At first the linguistic, formal, verbal mastery of literature, its critical examination, even its elocution, should remain in the background both for teacher and children. Let the direct impress of the thought, motive, and emotion of the characters be unimpeded; give the author a chance to speak direct to the hearts of the children, and the avenue toward the desired results in formal reading will be left wide open.

We would not deny that a certain labor is required of the teacher in such preparation. But, in the main, it is a refreshing kind of labor. If it brings a feeling of weariness, it is the kind that conduces to sound and healthy sleep. It invokes a feeling of inward power and of accumulated rich resource that helps us to meet with confidence the emergencies and opportunities of instruction.

2. In the assignment of the lesson the teacher has a chance to give the children a glimpse of the pleasure that awaits them, and to catch a little of the enthusiasm which her own study has awakened. This should be done briefly and by significant suggestion. In first introducing a longer work, it will pay to occupy more than is usual in recitations in opening up the new subject; if it is historical, in locating the time, circumstances, and geographical setting. The chief aim of the assignment should be to awaken curiosity and interest which may be strong enough to lead to a full and appreciative study of the lesson. A second aim of the assignment is to pave the way to an easier mastery of verbal difficulties that arise, such as new and difficult words, obscure or involved passages. The first aim is a substantial and fruitful one. It approaches the whole reading lesson from the side of interest and spirit. It seeks to plant direct incentives and suggestions deep enough in the mind to start effort. The assignment should take it for granted that natural interest and absorption in the thought will lead directly to that kind of vigorous effort and mastery that will secure natural and expressive oral reading. Look well to the deeper springs of thought and action, and the formal reading will open just the avenue needed to realize good expression.

Skill, originality, and teaching art are much needed in the assignment. It is not how much the teacher says, but the suggestiveness of it, the problems raised, the questions whose answers lie in the examination of the lesson. The reference to previous readings which bear resemblance to this selection; the inquiry into children's experiences, sets them to thinking.

Sometimes it pays to spend five or ten minutes in attacking the difficult words and meanings of the lesson assigned. Let the class read on and discover words or phrases that puzzle them. Let difficult forms be put on the board and syllabicated if necessary. A brief study of synonymous words and phrases may be in place.

It is a mistake to decline all helpful and suggestive study of the next lesson in class, on the ground that it invalidates the self-activity of children. Self-activity is, indeed, the chief aim of a good assignment. It is designed to stimulate the children to energetic and well-directed effort. Self-activity is not encouraged by requiring children to struggle with obstacles they have not the ability to surmount. Pronouncing new words and searching for dictionary meanings is often made a mechanical labor which is irksome and largely fruitless, because the wrong pronunciations are learned and the definitions do not fit. Before children are required to use the dictionary in pronouncing and defining words, they need careful exercises in how to use and to interpret the dictionary.

The teacher needs to make a study of the art of assigning lessons. Clearness and simplicity, so as to give no ground for misunderstandings, are the result of thoughtful preparation on the teacher's part. There is always danger of giving too much or too little, of carelessness and unsteady requirements, overburdening the children one day, and even forgetting the next day to assign a definite task. The forethought and precision with which a teacher assigns her lessons is one of the best tests of her prudence and success in teaching.

It is necessary also to be on one's guard against hasty assignments. Even when proper care has been taken in planning the next lesson, the time slips by with urgent work, and the signal for dismissal comes before time has been taken for any clear assignment.

If the teacher knows just what references will throw added light upon the lesson, what books and pages will be directly helpful, if he can appoint different pupils to look up particular references and sometimes even go to the library with them and search for the references, in grades from the fifth through the eighth, the result may be very helpful. In the class recitation it is necessary to gather up the fruits of this reference work with as little waste of time as possible, recognizing that it is purely collateral to the main purpose.

Pictures and maps are useful oftentimes as references. As children advance in the grades, they are capable of greater independence and judgment in the use of such materials. General, loose, and indefinite references are a sign of ignorance, carelessness, and lack of preparation on the teacher's part. They are discouraging and unprofitable to children. But we desire to see children broadening their views, extending their knowledge of books and of how to use them. The amount of good literature that can be well treated and read in the class is small, but much suggestive outside home and vacation reading may be encouraged, that will open a still wider and richer area of personal study.

3. In spite of all the precautions of the teacher, in spite of lively interest and intelligent study by the children, there will be many haltings and blunders, many inaccuracies in the use of eye and voice. These faults spring partly from habit and previous home influences. The worst faults are often those of which a child is unconscious, so habitual have they become. If we are to meet these difficulties wisely, we must start and keep up a strong momentum in the class. There should be a steady and strong current of effort in which all share. This depends, as has been often said, upon the power of the selection to awaken the thought and feeling of the children. It depends equally upon the pervasive spirit and energy of the teacher. If we try to analyze this complex phenomenon, we may find that, so far as the children are concerned, two elements are present, natural and spontaneous absorption in the ideas and sensibilities awakened by the author, and the bracing conviction that sustained effort is expected and required by the teacher. Children, to read well, must be free; they must feel the force of ideas and of the emotions and convictions awakened by them. They must also be conscious of that kind of authority and control which insists upon serious and sustained effort. Freedom to exercise their own powers and obedience to a controlling influence are needful. If the teacher can secure this right movement and ferment in a class, she will be able to correct the errors and change bad habits into the desired form of expression. The correction of errors, in the main, should be quiet, incidental, suggestive, not disturbing the child's thought and effort, not destroying the momentum of his sentiment and feeling. Let him move on firmly and vigorously; only direct his movement here and there, modify his tone by easy suggestions and pertinent questions, and encourage him as far as possible in his own effort to appreciate and express the author's idea.

In reading lessons there are certain purely formal exercises that are very helpful. The single and concert pronunciation of difficult or unusual words that come up in old and new lessons, the vocal exercises in syllabication and in vowel and consonant drill, are examples. They should be quick and vigorous, and preliminary to their application in lessons.

4. The teacher is only a guide and interpreter. With plenty of reserve power, he should only draw upon it occasionally. His chief business is not to show the children how to read by example, nor to be always explaining and amplifying the thought of the author. His aim should be to best call the minds of the children into strong action through the stimulation of the author's thought, and to go a step farther and reproduce and mould this thought into oral expression.

In order to call out the best efforts of children, a teacher needs to study well the art of questioning. The range of possibilities in questioning is very wide. If a rational, sensible question is regarded as the central or zero point, there are many degrees below it in the art of questioning and many degrees above it. Below it is a whole host of half-rational or useless questions which would better be left unborn: What does this word mean? Why didn't you study your lesson? Why weren't you paying attention? What is the definition of also? How many mistakes did Mary make?

Much time is sometimes wasted in trying to answer aimless or trivial questions: Peter, what does this strange word mean, or how do you pronounce it? Ethel may try it. Who thinks he can pronounce it better? Johnny, try it. Perhaps somebody knows how it ought to be. Sarah, can't you pronounce it? Finally, after various efforts, the teacher passes on to something else without even making clear the true pronunciation or meaning. This is worse than killing time. It is befuddling the children. A question should aim clearly at some important idea, and should bring out a definite result. The children should have time to think, but not to guess and dawdle, and then be left groping in the dark.

The chief aim of questions is to arouse vigor and variety of thought as a means of better appreciation and expression. Children read poorly because they do not see the meaning or do not feel the force of the sentiment. They give wrong emphasis and intonation. A good question is like a flash of lightning which suddenly reveals our standing-ground and surroundings, and gives the child a chance to strike out again for himself. His intelligence lights up, he sees the point, and responds with a significant rendering of the thought. But the teacher must be a thinker to ask simple and pertinent questions. He can't go at it in a loose and lumbering fashion. Lively and sympathetic and appreciative of the child's moods and feelings must he be, as well as clear and definite in his own perception of the author's meaning.

Questioning for meaning is equivalent to that for securing expression, and thus two birds are hit with one stone. A pointed question energizes thought along a definite line, and leads to a more intense and vivid perception of the meaning. This is just the vantage-ground we desire in order to secure good expression. We wish children not to imitate, but first to see and feel, and then to express in becoming wise the thought as they see it and feel it. This makes reading a genuine performance, not a parrot-like formalism.

5. Trying to awaken the mental energy and action of a class as they move on through a masterpiece, requires constant watchfulness to keep alive their sense-perceptions and memories, and to touch their imaginations into constructive effort at every turn in the road. Through the direct action of the senses the children have accumulated much variety of sense-materials, of country and town, of hill, valley, river, lake, fields, buildings, industries, roads, homes, gardens, seasons. Out of this vast and varied quarry they are able to gather materials with which to construct any landscape or situation you may desire. Give the children abundance of opportunity to use these collected riches, and to construct, each in his own way, the scenes and pictures that the poet's art so vividly suggests. Many of the questions we ask of children are designed simply to recall and reawaken images which lie dormant in their minds, or, on the other hand, to find out whether they can combine their old sense-perceptions so skilfully and vividly as to realize the present situation. Keen and apt questions will reach down into the depth of a child's life experiences and bring up concrete images which the fancy then modifies and adjusts to the present need. The teacher may often suggest something in his own observations to kindle like memories in theirs. Or, if the subject seems unfamiliar, he may bring on a picture from book or magazine. Sometimes a sketch or diagram on the board may give sense-precision and definiteness to the object discussed, even though it be rudely drawn. This constant appeal to what is real and tangible and experimental, not only locates things definitely in time and space, makes clear and plain

what was hazy or meaningless, awakens interest by connecting the story or description with former experiences, but it sets in action the creative imagination which shapes and builds up new and pleasing structures, combining old and new. This kind of mental elaboration, which reaches back into the senses and forward into the imagination, is what gives mobility and adjustability to our mental resources. It is not stiff and rigid and refractory knowledge that we need. Ideas may retain their truth and strength, their inward quality, and still submit to infinite variations and adjustments. Water is one of the most serviceable of all nature's compounds, because it has such mobility of form, such capacity to dissolve and take into solution other substances, or of being absorbed and even lost sight of in other bodies. The ideas we have gathered and stored up from all sources are our building materials; the imagination is the architect who conceives the plan and directs the use of different materials in the growth of the new structures. The teacher's chief function in reading classes is, on the one hand, to see that children revive and utilize their sense-knowledge, and on the other, to wake the sleeping giant and set him to work to build the beauteous structures for which the materials have been prepared. But for this, teachers could be dispensed with. As Socrates said, they are only helpers; they stand by, not to perform the work, but to gently guide, to stimulate, and now and then to lend a helping hand over a bad place.

Explanations, therefore, on the teacher's part, should be clear and brief, purely tributary to the main effort. In younger classes, when the children have, as yet, little ability to use references, the teacher may add much, especially if it be concrete, graphic, picturesque, and bearing directly upon the subject. But as children grow more self-reliant they can look up facts and references, and bring more material themselves to the elucidation of the lesson. But even in adult classes the rich experience of a trained and wise teacher, whose illustrations are apt and graphic and criticisms incisive, is an intense pleasure and stimulus to students.

6. The major part of time and effort in reading classes should be given to the reading proper, and not to oral discussions, explanations, and collateral information and references. It is possible to have interesting discussions and much use of reference books, and still make small progress in expressive reading. The main thing should not be lost sight of. We should learn to march steadily forward through lively and energetic thought toward

expressive reading. There is no other right approach to good reading except through a lively grasp of the thought, sentiment, and style of the author. But the side-lights that come from collateral reading and reference are of great significance. They are something like the scenery on the stage. They make the effect more intense and real. They supply a background of environment and association which give the ideas more local significance and a stronger basis in the whole complex of ideas.

The reading or oral rendering is the final test of understanding and appreciation of the lesson. The recitation should focus in this applied art. All questioning and discussion that do not eventuate in expressive reading fall short of their proper result. Reading is a school exercise in which the principles discussed can be immediately applied, and this is scarcely true in studies like history, science, and mathematics. There are many hindrances in the way of this fruitful result; the teacher is tempted to talk and explain too much, interesting questions and controversies spring up, trivial matters receive too much consideration, much time is spent in the oral reproduction of the thought; often the time slips by with a minimum of effective reading.

The questions, discussions, collateral references, and explanations should be brought into immediate connection with the children's reading, so that the special thought may produce its effect upon expression. This test of effectiveness is a good one to apply to explanations, definitions, and questions. Unless they produce a pronounced effect upon the reading, they are largely superfluous. In view of this the teacher will learn to be sparing of words, laconic and definite in statement, pointed and clear in questioning, and energetic in pushing forward. While interest in the thought-content is the impelling motive in good reading exercises, lively and natural expression is likewise the proper fruit and outcome of such a motive carried to its proper end.

7. In order to keep up the right interest and movement, it is necessary to give considerable variety to the work. A teacher's good sense and tact should be like a thermometer which registers the mental temperature of the class. If kept too long at a single line of effort, its monotony induces carelessness and inattention; while a total change to some other order of exercise would awake their interest and zeal. Variety is needed also within the compass of a single recitation, because there are several preliminaries

and varieties of preparatory drill which conduce to good rendering of any selection. Such are vocal exercises in consonants and vowels; pronunciation and syllabication of new or difficult words; physical exercises to put the body and nervous system into proper tone; the assignment of the next lesson, requiring a peculiar effort and manner of treatment; the report and discussion of references; concert drills; the study of meanings—synonyms and derivations; illustrations and information by the teacher; introduction of other illustrative matter, as pictures, drawings, maps, and diagrams. Variety can be given to each lesson in many ways according to the ingenuity of the teacher. If we are reading a number of short selections, they themselves furnish different varieties and types of prose and verse. The dramatist or novelist provides for such variety by introducing a series of diverse scenes, all leading forward to a common end.

8. Parallel to the requirement of variety is the equally important demand that children should learn to do one thing at a time and learn to do it well. This may appear contradictory to the former requirement, but the skill and tact of the teacher is what should solve this seeming contradiction. It is a fact that we try to do too many things in each reading lesson. We fail to pound on one nail long enough to drive it in. Reading lessons often resemble a child pounding nails into a board. He strikes one nail a blow or two, then another, and so on until a dozen or more are in all stages of incompleteness. We too often allow the recitation hour to end with a number of such incomplete efforts. Good reading is not like moving a house, when it is all carried along in one piece. We reach better results if we concentrate attention and effort during a recitation along the line of a narrow aim. At least this seems true of the more formal, mechanical side of reading. It is better to try to break up bad habits, one at a time, rather than to make a general, indefinite onslaught upon all together. Suppose, for example, that the teacher suggests as an aim of the lesson conversational reading, or that which sounds like pupils talking to each other. Many dialogue selections admit of such an aim as this. If this aim is set up at the beginning of the lesson, the children's minds will be rendered acute in this direction; they will be on the alert for this kind of game. Each child who reads is scrutinized by teacher and pupils to see how near he comes to the ideal. A conscious effort begins to dominate the class to reach this specific goal. Children may close their eyes and listen to see if the reading has the

right sound. A girl or boy goes into an adjoining entry or dressing room and listens to see if those in the class are reading or talking. The enthusiasm and class spirit awakened are very helpful. Not that a whole recitation should be given up to that sort of thing, but it is the characteristic effort of the lesson. When the children practise the next lesson at home they will have this point in mind.

For several days this sort of specific, definite aim at a narrow result may be followed up in the class till the children begin to acquire power in this direction. What was, at first, painfully conscious effort begins to assume the form of habit, and when this result is achieved, we may drop this aim as a leading one in the recitation, and turn our attention to some different line of effort. Distinct pronunciation of sounds is one of the things that we are always aiming at, in a general way, and never getting. Why not set this up in a series of recitations as a definite aim, and resort to a series of devices to lay bare the kind of faults the children are habitually guilty of? Give them a chance to correct these faults, and awake the class spirit in this direction. It will not be difficult to convince them that they are not pronouncing their final consonants, like *d, t, l, m, r,* and *k*. Keep the attention for a lesson to this kind of error till there is recognizable improvement. Then notice the short vowel sounds in the unaccented syllables, and give them search-light attention. Notice later the syllables that children commonly slur over. Mark these fugitives, and see if they continue so invisible and inaudible. They are like Jack the Giant Killer, when he put on his cloak of invisibility, or like Perseus under similar circumstances. See if we can find these fellows who seem to masquerade and dodge about behind their companions. Then some of the long vowels and diphthongs will require investigation. They are not all so open-faced and above board as they might be. When children have such a simple and distinct aim in view, they are ready to work with a vim and to exert themselves in a conscious effort at improvement. Keep this aim foremost in the recitation, although other requirements of good reading are not wholly neglected.

After a definite line of effort has been strongly developed as one of the above described, it is possible thereafter to keep it in mind with slight attention. But if no special drill has ever been devoted to it for a given length of time, it has not been brought so distinctly to mind as to produce a lasting impression and to lay the basis for habit. Besides the two aims, clear articulation and conversational tones, there are others that may be labored at similarly. Appreciation of the thought as expressed by the reading is a rich field for critical study of a piece, and as a basis for observing and judging the children's reading. This idea is well implied by such questions as follow: Is that what the passage means? Have you given expression to the author's meaning by emphasis on this word? Does your rendering of this passage make good sense? Compare it with what precedes. How did the man feel when he said this? What do we know of his character that would lead us to expect such words from him? This line of questions has a wide and varied range. The chief thing is to scrutinize the thought in all the light attainable, and appeal to the child's own judgment as to the suitableness of the tone and emphasis to the thought. Does it sound right? Is that what the passage means?

Each characteristic form of prose or verse has a peculiar style and force of expression that calls for a corresponding oral rendering. There is the serious and massive, though simple, diction of Webster's speeches, with its smooth and rounded periods, calling for slow and steady and energetic reading. We should notice this characteristic of an author, and grow into sympathy with his feeling, language, and mental movement. In Macaulay's "Lays of Ancient Rome," the ring of martial music is in the words, and it swells out into rapid and rousing speech which should correspond to the thought. In "Evangeline" the flow of language is placid and gentle and rhythmical, and in consonance with the gentle faith and hope of Evangeline. Every true literary product has its own character, which the genius of the author has impressed upon its language and moulded into its structure, and which calls for a rendering fit and appropriate. Before completing a selection, we should detect this essence and quality and bring our reading to reveal it. The places should be pointed out where it comes into prominence.

When completing such a work of art there should be given opportunity to bring all the varied elements and special aims discovered and worked out during its reading to a focus.

In the final review and rereading of a complete poem or prose selection the points of excellence in reading which have been the special aims of effort in the studies of the piece should be kept sharply in mind and pushed to a full expression. The realization of these various aims may be set before the class as the distinct object of their closing work on a masterpiece. The failure to hold vigorously to this final achievement is a clear sign of intellectual and moral lassitude. Reading, as noticed before, is one of the few studies in which the final application of theory to practice can be effected, and children may realize that things are learned for the sake of using them, and not simply against some future contingency. This implies, however, much resource and skill on the teacher's part in awakening the children. The impulses and aims which arouse the children to strenuous effort should spring from within, and should be expressions of their own self-activity and volition. There is much need of the enthusiasm and will-energy that overcome drudgery. Children should be taught to be dissatisfied with anything less than real accomplishment.

The children will naturally memorize certain passages which strike their fancy. Other passages have been suggested by the teacher for different pupils to memorize. In one of the closing lessons let the children recite these parts before the class. If the teacher has succeeded in calling out the live interest of the class during the previous study, such a lesson will be a joy to both pupils and teacher. One or two of the children may also volunteer or be appointed to make an oral statement of the argument, which will give freedom to natural and effective speech. Such a round-up of the reading lessons at the end of a series of interesting studies is a rich experience to the whole class.

Besides the important special aims thus far suggested, which should each stand out clear for a series of lessons until its value is realized and worked over into habit, there are other subordinate aims that deserve particular and individual consideration, and may now and then become the dominant purpose of a lesson. Such are the correction of singsong reading, the use of the dictionary, the study of synonyms and antitheses, the comparisons and figures of speech, exercises in sight reading of unfamiliar selections, quotations from selections and masterpieces already read, study of the lives and works of authors.

Reading is a many-sided study, and to approach its difficulties with success we must take them up one at a time, conquering them in detail. Good housekeepers and cooks are accustomed to lay out a series of dinners in which the chief article of diet is varied from day to day as follows:

chicken pie with oysters, veal potpie, stewed fish, broiled beefsteak, venison roast, bean soup with ham, roast mutton, baked fish, broiled quail, roast beef, baked chicken with parsnips, etc. Such a series of dinners gives a healthy variety and relish. It is better for most people than the bill of fare at a large hotel, where there is so much variety and sameness each day. When we try each day to do everything in a reading lesson, we grasp more than our hands can hold, and most of it falls to the ground. Children are pleased and encouraged by actual progress in surmounting difficulties when they are presented one at a time, and opportunity is given for complete mastery. The children should labor consciously and vigorously at one line of effort, be it distinctness or rhythm or emphasis or conversational tone, till decided improvement and progress are attained, and the ease of right habit begins to show itself. Then we can turn to some new field, securing and holding the vantage-ground of our foregoing effort by occasional reminders.

9. One of the best tests applied to a reading class is their degree of class attention. The steadiness and responsiveness with which the whole class follow the work is a fair measure of successful teaching. To have but one child read at a time while the others wait their turn or scatter their thoughts, is very bad. It is a good sign of a teacher's skill and efficiency to see every child in energetic pursuit of the reading. It conduces to the best progress in that study and is the genesis of right mental habit.

Attention is a *sine qua non* to good teaching, and yet it is a result rather than a cause. It is a ripe fruit rather than the spring promise of it. The provisions which lead up to steady attention are deserving of a teacher's study and patient scrutiny. She may command attention for a moment by sheer force of will and personality, but it must have something to feed upon the next moment and the next, or it will be wandering in distant fields. So great and indispensable is the value of attention, that some teachers try to secure it at too heavy a cost. They command, threaten, punish. They resort to severity and cruelty. But the more formidable the teacher becomes, the more difficult for a child to do his duty. Here, again, we can best afford to go back to the sources from which attention naturally springs, interesting subject of thought, vivid and concrete perceptions, lively and suggestive appeal to the imagination, the sphere of noble thought and emotion, variety and movement in mental effort, a mutual sympathy and harmony between teacher and pupil.

It is indeed well for the teacher to gauge his work by the kind and intensity of attention he can secure. If the class has dropped into slothful and habitual carelessness and inattention, he will have to give them a few severe jolts; he must drop questions where they are least expected. He must be very alert to detect a listless child and wake him into action. The vigor, personal will, and keen watchfulness of the teacher must be a constant resource. On the other hand, let him look well to the thought, the feeling, and capacity of the children, and give them matter which is equal to their merits.

It is not unusual to find the teacher's eye following the text closely instead of watching the class. But the teacher's eye should be moving alertly among the children. In case he has studied the lesson carefully, the teacher can detect almost every mistake without the book. In fact, even if one has not recently read a selection, he can usually detect a verbal error by the break or incoherency of the thought. Moreover, the teacher can better judge the expressiveness of the reading by listening to it than by following the text with his eye. Depending wholly upon the ear, any defect of utterance or ineptness of expression is quickly detected. Even the children at times should be asked to close their books and to listen closely to the reading. This emphasizes the notion that good reading is the oral expression of thought, so that those who listen can understand and enjoy it.

The treadmill style of reading, which repeats and repeats, doing the same things day by day, going through the like round of mechanical motions, should give way to a rational, spirited, variegated method which arouses interest and variety of thought, and moves ever toward a conscious goal.

10. In studying the masterpieces of great writers, a question arises how to treat the moral situations involved in the stories. In their revolt against excessive moralizing with children, some critics object to any direct teaching of moral ideas in connection with literature, being opposed to explicit discussions of moral notions.

All will admit that literature, dealing as it does with human life, is surcharged with practical morality, with social conduct. It is also the motive of great writers, while dealing honestly with human nature, to idealize and beautify their representations of men. Nor is it their purpose to make unworthy characters pleasing and attractive models.

It is expected, of course, that children will get clear notions and opinions of such persons as Miles Standish and John Alden, of Whittier's father and mother and others in the fireside circle of "Snow-Bound," of Antonio and Shylock in the "Merchant of Venice," of Cinderella and her sisters in the story, of Wallace and Bruce in Scott's "Tales," of Gluck and his brothers in Ruskin's story, of Scrooge in the "Christmas Carol," of Evangeline, Enoch Arden, etc.

But boys and girls are not infallible judges of character. They are apt to form erroneous or one-sided judgments from lack of insight into the author's meaning, or from carelessness. There is the same possibility of error in forming moral judgments as in forming judgments in other phases of an author's thought.

It is the province of the teacher to stimulate the children to think, and, by his superior experience and judgment, to guide them into correct thinking. It is not the function of the teacher to impose his ready-made judgments upon children, either in morals or in anything else. But it is his concern, by questions, suggestions, and criticisms, to aid in clarifying the thought, to put the children upon the right track. There is no reason why a teacher should abdicate his place of instructor because he chances to come before moral problems. Literature is full of moral situations, moral problems, and moral evolutions in character, and even of moral ideals. Is the teacher to stand dumb before these things as if he had lost his wits? Or is he to consider it the greatest opportunity of his life to prudently guide young people to the correct perception of what is beautiful and true in human life? Why, indeed, should he suppress his own enthusiasm for these ideals? Why should not his personality be free to express itself in matters of moral concern, as well as in intellectual and æsthetic judgments? So long as the teacher throws the pupils back upon their own self-activity and thinking power, there need be no danger of moral pedantry or of moral dyspepsia.

It seems to me, therefore, that the teacher should use freedom and boldness in discussing with the children candidly and thoughtfully the characters presented in good literature. Let the situations be made clear so that correct judgments of single acts can be formed. Let the weaknesses and virtues of the persons be noted. Let motives be studied and characteristic tendencies traced out. In this way children may gradually increase their insight and enlarge the range of their knowledge of social life. If these things are not legitimate, why should such materials be presented to children at all? We need not make premature moralists of children, or teach them to pass easy or flippant moral judgments upon others. But we wish their interest in these characters to be deep and genuine, their eyes wide open to the truths of life, and their intuitive moral judgments to ripen in a healthy and hearty social environment. To this end the teacher will need to use all his skill in questioning, in suggestion, in frank and candid discussion. In short, he needs just those qualities which a first-class teacher needs in any field of study.

We have gotten out of the mode of tacking a moral to a story. Ostensibly moral stories, overweighted with a moral purpose, do not please us. We wish novelists and dramatists to give us the truth of life, and leave us to pass judgment upon the characters. Our best literature presents great variety of scenes and characterizations in their natural setting in life. They specially cultivate moral judgment and insight. One of the ultimate standards which we apply to all novels and dramas is that of their fundamental moral truth. Schlegel, in his "Dramatic Art and Literature," in his criticisms of great writers, discusses again and again the moral import of the characters, and even the moral purpose of Shakespeare and the dramatists. In fact, these moral considerations lie deep and fundamental in judging the great works of literary art. The masterpieces we use in the schools bear the same relation to the children that the more difficult works bear to adults.

The clear discussion of the moral element in literature seems, therefore, natural and legitimate, while its neglect and obscuration would be a fatal defect.

11. There are two kinds of reading which should be cultivated in reading lessons, although they seem to fall a little apart from the main highway of effort. They are, first, sight reading of supplementary matter for the purpose of cultivating a quick and accurate grasp of new thought and forms. When we leave school, one of the values of reading will be the power it gives to interpret quickly and grasp firmly the ideas as they present themselves in

the magazines, papers, and books we read. Good efforts in school reading will lead forward gradually to that readiness of thought and fluency of perception which will give freedom and mastery of new reading matter. To develop this ability and to regulate it into habit, we must give children a chance to read quite a little at sight. We need supplementary readers in sets which can be put into the hands of children for this purpose. The same books will answer for several classes, and may be passed from room to room of similar grade.

The reading matter we select for this purpose may be classic, and of the best quality, just as well as to be limited to information and geographical readers which are much inferior. There are first-class books of literary merit, which are entirely serviceable for this purpose and much richer in culture. They continue the line of study in classic literature, and give ground for suggestive comparisons and reviews which should not be neglected. There is a strong tendency in our time to put inferior reading matter, in the form of information readers, science primers, short history stories, geographical readers, newspapers, and specially prepared topics on current events, into reading classes. These things may do well enough in their proper place in geography, history, natural science, or general lessons, but they should appear scarcely at all in reading lessons. Preserve the reading hour for that which is choicest in our prose and verse, mainly in the form of shorter or longer masterpieces of literature.

Secondly, many books should be brought to the attention of the children which they may read outside of school. The regular reading exercises should give the children a lively and attractive introduction to some of the best authors, and a taste for the strength and beauty of their productions. But the field of literature is so wide and varied that many things can only be suggested, which will remain for the future leisure and choice of readers. Children might, however, be made acquainted with some of the best books suited to their age for which there is not school time. Many of the best books, like "Ivanhoe," "Quentin Durward," "Captains Courageous," "Swiss Family Robinson," and "Nicholas Nickleby," cannot be read in school. They should be in the school library, and the teacher should often refer to them and to others suggested by the regular reading, which give deeper and wider views into life.

12. In the use of the symbols and language forms of reading, the children should be led on to freedom and self-activity. How to get the mastery of these forms in the early reading work is discussed in the "Special Method in Primary Reading and Story."

In the fourth and fifth years of school, children should learn to use the dictionary. It is a great means of self-help when they have learned to interpret the dictionary easily. But special lessons are necessary to teach children: first, how to find words in the dictionary; second, how to interpret the diacritical markings so as to get a correct pronunciation; and third, how to discriminate among definitions. Adults and even teachers are often deficient in these particulars, and children will not form habits of using the dictionary with quick and easy confidence without continuous, attentive care on the teacher's part. The best outcome of such training is the conscious power of the child to help himself, and there is nothing in school work more deserving of encouragement.

The system of diacritical markings used in the dictionary should be put on the blackboard, varied illustrations of the markings given, and the application of these markings to new words in the dictionary discovered. Lack of success in this work is chiefly due to a failure to pursue this plan steadily till ease and mastery are gained and habits formed.

In the later grades these habits of self-help should be kept up and extended further to the study of synonyms, root words and their kindred, homonyms, prefixes and suffixes, and the derived meanings of words.

CHAPTER V

METHOD FURTHER DISCUSSED AND ILLUSTRATED. SUMMARY

In the following chapter some phases of method not fully treated before will be discussed and illustrated.

1. The proposal to treat literary masterpieces as units of thought implies a searching study and sifting out of the essential idea in each poem or selection. In some, both of the longer and shorter pieces, it is not difficult to detect the motive. In Bryant's "Ode to a Waterfowl," it is even suggested as a sort of moral at the close. Likewise in the "Pied Piper of Hamelin," and in Burns's "Tam O'Shanter." In "Glaucis and Philemon," as well as in "The Golden Touch," even a child can quickly discern the controlling idea of the myth. But in many of our choicest literary products it requires deliberate thought to discover the poet's deeper meaning, especially that idea which binds all the parts together and gives unity to the whole. In Lowell's address "To the Dandelion," we may find in each stanza the gleam of the golden thread which unifies the whole. The first lines suggest it:—

> "Dear common flower, that grow'st beside the way,
> Fringing the dusty road with harmless gold."

And again in the second stanza:—

> "'Tis the Spring's largess which she scatters now
> To rich and poor alike, with lavish hand."

In the succeeding stanzas he calls to mind how the dandelion suggests the riches of the tropics, the full promise of summer, the pure joys of childhood, the common loving courtesies of life, the rich love and prodigality of nature, and the divinity in every human heart.

When by reflection we bind all these thoughts together, and find that they focus in the idea that the best riches abound and even burst forth out of common things and from the hearts of common men and women, we realize that the poet has brought us to the point of discovering a deep and practical truth, which, put to work in the world, would bring rhythm and harmony into human life.

But such a deep impression is not made by a superficial or fragmental study of the poem.

A somewhat similar result may be wrought out by the study of Lowell's poem, "An Incident in a Railroad Car," and the idea is well expressed in the verse:—

> "Never did poesy appear
> So full of heaven to me as when
> I saw how it would pierce through pride and fear
> To lives of coarsest men."

The study of a poem or other masterpiece in this way, to get at its inner life and continuity, reveals to us an interesting process of mental elaboration and comparative thought. Such self-active reflection is the subsoiling of the mind.

To set children to work upon problems of this sort, to put them in the way of thinking and feeling for themselves, and that too even in the longer classics like "Evangeline," "Enoch Arden," "Silas Marner," etc., is to bring such studies into the realm of great culture-producing agencies.

Many minor questions of method will be solved by having these centres of thought, these problems for thinkers. Teachers are bothered to know what sort of questions to ask. It would be safe to say, those questions which move in the direction of the main truth, toward the solution of the chief problem. But let the questions be shrewd, not revealing too much, stimulating to thoughtfulness and heading off errors. To what extent shall geographical, historical, or biographical facts be gathered for the enrichment and clarifying of the poem? Those materials which throw necessary light on the essential ideas, omitting what is irrelevant and secondary.

A careful study of the life of Alexander, by Plutarch, will bring to light, more than anything else, his magnanimity. The thing that so much distinguished him from other men was his large, liberal temper, displayed on many various occasions. It reminds the mature student of that remarkable utterance of Burke, "Great affairs and little minds go ill together." The large-minded statesmanship with which Burke discusses conciliation with the colonies is of like quality with this magnanimous spirit of Alexander.

One who reads receptively Emerson's "The Fortune of the Republic" will open his eyes on two opposite but closely related ideas, the serious faults,— the low political tone, the materialism, the spread-eagle strut and slovenly mediocrity of much in American life,—and over against this the splendid promise, manliness, and intense idealism of our national life. To work out this conception in the brains of young people and let it kindle their hearts with some true glow of patriotism, is the highest form of teaching. Such instruction would convert every schoolhouse into a true temple of freedom and patriotism.

But in order to reach these results both teachers and pupils must put their minds to the stretch of earnest work. In the introduction to the above-named essay of Emerson, in the "Riverside Literature Series," occurs the following interesting and suggestive passage: "Yet many of his most notable addresses were given before audiences of young men and women, and out of the great body of his writings it is not difficult to find many passages which go straight to the intelligence of boys and girls in school. The plan of this series forbids the use of extracts, or many numbers might be filled with striking and appropriate passages from Emerson's writings; but there are certain essays and addresses which, though they may contain some knotty sentences, are in the main so interesting to boys and girls who have begun to think, they are so inspiring and yield so much to any one who will take a little trouble to use his mind, that it is obviously desirable to bring them in convenient form to the attention of schools. Some of the best things in literature we can get only by digging for them; and there is great satisfaction in reading again and again masterpieces like the essays in this collection, with a fresh pleasure in each reading as new ideas spring up in the mind of the attentive reader."

It will be a day rich in promise and fruitful of great things when the general body of our teachers take hold of our great American classics in this determined spirit, treating them as wholes and grasping firmly the essential fundamental ideas.

2. It is in the thought-analysis of a reading lesson that a teacher's wit and wisdom are brought to the severest test. The words of Shakespeare may be applied to the teacher:—

> "A prince most prudent, of an excellent
> And unmatched wit and judgment."

There is much danger of wasting time in formal questions, questions striking no spark of interest, questions on familiar words that really need no elucidation, vague and unpremeditated questions that make no forward step. Simple, far-reaching questions, which touch the pupils' deeper thoughtfulness in preparing the lesson and stimulate his self-active effort, are needed. If the teacher has become keenly interested, he will ask more telling questions. If he has probed into the author's secret,—the thing which he has been hinting at and only gives occasional glimpses of to whet your curiosity,—he will discover that thought-getting is almost a tantalizing process with great writers. The teacher must spur and almost tantalize the children with a similar shrewdness of question.

Problem-raising questions, involving thoughtful retrospect and shrewd anticipation, questions which cannot be answered offhand but lead on to a deeper study, are at a premium. Ruskin says:—

"And, therefore, first of all, I tell you earnestly and authoritatively (I know I am right in this), you must get into the habit of looking intensely at words and assuring yourself of their meaning, syllable by syllable,—nay, letter by letter." Again he says, of a well-educated gentleman, that "above all he is learned in the peerage of words; knows the words of true descent and ancient blood at a glance from words of modern canaille."

In order to make his thought unmistakable, I quote at length a passage from Ruskin's "Sesame and Lilies":—

"And now, merely for example's sake, I will, with your permission, read a few lines of a true book with you, carefully; and see what will come out of them. I will take a book perfectly known to you all; no English words are more familiar to us, yet nothing perhaps has been less read with sincerity. I will take these few following lines of 'Lycidas':—

> "'Last came, and last did go,
> The pilot of the Galilean lake;
> Two massy keys he bore of metals twain,
> (The golden opes, the iron shuts amain),
> He shook his mitred locks, and stern bespake,
> How well could I have spar'd for thee, young swain,
> Enow of such as for their bellies' sake
> Creep and intrude, and climb into the fold:
> Of other care they little reckoning make,
> Than how to scramble at the shearers' feast,
> And shove away the worthy bidden guest;
> Blind mouths! that scarce themselves know how to hold
> A sheep-hook, or have learn'd aught else, the least
> That to the faithful herdsman's art belongs!
> What recks it them? What need they? They are sped;
> And when they list, their lean and flashy songs
> Grate on their scrannel pipes of wretched straw;
> The hungry sheep look up, and are not fed,

> But, swoln with wind, and the rank mist they draw,
> Rot inwardly, and foul contagion spread;
> Besides what the grim wolf with privy paw
> Daily devours apace, and nothing said.'

"Let us think over this passage, and examine its words.

"First, is it not singular to find Milton assigning to St. Peter, not only his full episcopal function, but the very types of it which Protestants usually refuse most passionately? His 'mitred' locks! Milton was no Bishop-lover; how comes St. Peter to be 'mitred'? 'Two massy keys he bore.' Is this, then, the power of the keys claimed by the Bishops of Rome, and is it acknowledged here by Milton only in a poetical license, for the sake of its picturesqueness; that he may get the gleam of the golden keys to help his effect? Do not think it. Great men do not play stage tricks with doctrines of life and death: only little men do that. Milton means what he says; and means it with his might, too,—is going to put the whole strength of his spirit presently into the saying of it. For though not a lover of false bishops, he was a lover of true ones; and the lake-pilot is here, in his thoughts, the type and head of true episcopal power. For Milton reads that text, 'I will give unto thee the keys of the kingdom of Heaven,' quite honestly. Puritan though he be, he would not blot it out of the book because there have been bad bishops; nay, in order to understand him, we must understand that verse first; it will not do to eye it askance, or whisper it under our breath, as if it were a weapon of an adverse sect. It is a solemn, universal assertion, deeply to be kept in mind by all sects. But perhaps we shall be better able to reason on it if we go on a little farther, and come back to it. For clearly, this marked insistence on the power of the true episcopate is to make us feel more weightily what is to be charged against the false claimants of episcopate; or generally, against false claimants of power and rank in the body of the clergy; they who, 'for their bellies' sake, creep, and intrude, and climb into the fold.'

"Do not think Milton uses those three words to fill up his verse, as a loose writer would. He needs all the three; specially those three, and no more than those—'creep,' and 'intrude,' and 'climb'; no other words would or could serve the turn, and no more could be added. For they exhaustively comprehend the three classes, correspondent to the three characters, of men who dishonestly seek ecclesiastical power. First, those who 'creep' into the fold; who do not care for office, nor name, but for secret influence, and do all things occultly and cunningly, consenting to any servility of office or conduct, so only that they may intimately discern, and unawares direct the minds of men. Then those who 'intrude' (thrust, that is) themselves into the fold, who by natural insolence of heart, and stout eloquence of tongue, and fearlessly perseverant self-assertion, obtain hearing and authority with the common crowd. Lastly, those who 'climb,' who by labor and learning, both stout and sound, but selfishly exerted in the cause of their own ambition, gain high dignities and authorities, and become 'lords over the heritage,' though not 'ensamples to the flock.'

"Now go on:—

> "'Of other care they little reckoning make,
> Than how to scramble at the shearers' feast.
> Blind mouths—'

"I pause again, for this is a strange expression; a broken metaphor, one might think, careless and unscholarly.

"Not so: its very audacity and pithiness are intended to make us look close at the phrase and remember it. Those two monosyllables express the precisely accurate contraries of right character, in the two great offices of the Church—those of bishop and pastor.

"A Bishop means a person who sees.

"A Pastor means one who feeds.

"The most unbishoply character a man can have is therefore to be Blind.

"The most unpastoral is, instead of feeding, to want to be fed,—to be a Mouth.

"Take the two reverses together, and you have 'blind mouths.' We may advisably follow out this idea a little. Nearly all the evils in the Church have arisen from bishops desiring power more than light. They want authority, not outlook. Whereas their real office is not to rule; though it may be vigorously to exhort and rebuke; it is the king's office to rule; the bishop's office is to oversee the flock; to number it, sheep by sheep; to be ready always to give full account of it. Now it is clear he cannot give account of the souls, if he has not so much as numbered the bodies of his flock. The first thing, therefore, that a bishop has to do is at least to put himself in a position in which, at any moment, he can obtain the history from childhood of every living soul in his diocese, and of its present state. Down in that back street, Bill, and Nancy, knocking each other's teeth out!—Does the bishop know all about it? Has he his eye upon them? Has he had his eye upon them? Can he circumstantially explain to us how Bill got into the habit of beating Nancy about the head? If he cannot, he is no bishop, though he had a mitre as high as Salisbury steeple; he is no bishop,—he has sought to be at the helm instead of the masthead; he has no sight of things. 'Nay,' you say, it is not his duty to look after Bill in the back street. What! the fat sheep that have full fleeces—you think it is only those he should look after, while (go back to your Milton) 'the hungry sheep look up, and are not fed, besides what the grim wolf with privy paw' (bishops knowing nothing about it) 'daily devours apace, and nothing said'?

"'But that's not our idea of a bishop.' Perhaps not; but it was St. Paul's; and it was Milton's. They may be right, or we may be; but we must not think we are reading either one or the other by putting our meaning into their words.

"I go on.

"'But, swolln with wind, and the rank mist they draw.'

"This is to meet the vulgar answer that 'if the poor are not looked after in their bodies, they are in their souls; they have spiritual food.'

"And Milton says, 'They have no such thing as spiritual food; they are only swolln with wind.' At first you may think that is a coarse type, and an obscure one. But, again, it is a quite literally accurate one. Take up your Latin and Greek dictionaries, and find out the meaning of 'Spirit.' It is only a contraction of the Latin word 'breath,' and an indistinct translation of the Greek word for 'wind.' The same word is used in writing. 'The wind bloweth where it listeth;' and 'So is every one that is born of the Spirit,' born of the breath, that is, for it means the breath of God, in soul and body. We have the true sense of it in our words 'inspiration' and 'expire.' Now, there are two kinds of breath with which the flock may be filled; God's breath and man's. The breath of God is health and life and peace to them, as the air of heaven is to the flocks on the hills; but man's breath—the word he calls spiritual—is disease and contagion to them, as the fog of the fen. They rot inwardly with it; they are puffed up by it, as a body by the vapors of its own decomposition. This is literally true of all false religious teaching; the first and last and fatalest sign of it is that 'puffing up.'

"Lastly, let us return to the lines respecting the power of the keys, for now we can understand them. Note the difference between Milton and Dante in their interpretation of this power; for once the latter is weaker in thought; he supposes both the keys to be of the gate of heaven; one is of gold, the other of silver; they are given by St. Peter to the sentinel angel, and it is not easy to determine the meaning either of the substances of the three steps of the gate or of the two keys. But Milton makes one, of gold, the key of heaven; the other, of iron, the key of the prison, in which the wicked teachers are to be bound who 'have taken away the key of knowledge, yet entered not in themselves.'

"We have seen that the duties of bishop and pastor are to see and feed, and, of all who do so, it is said, 'He that watereth, shall be watered also himself.' But the reverse is truth also. He that watereth not, shall be withered himself, and he that seeth not, shall himself be shut out of sight,— shut into the perpetual prison house. And that prison opens here as well as hereafter; he who is to be bound in heaven must first be bound on earth. That command to the strong angels, of which the rock-apostle is the image, 'Take him, and bind him hand and foot, and cast him out,' issues, in its measure, against the teacher for every help withheld, and for every truth refused, and for every falsehood enforced; so that he is more strictly fettered the more he fetters, and further outcast as he more and more misleads, till at last the bars of the iron cage close upon him, and as 'the golden opes, the iron shuts amain.'

"We have got something out of the lines, I think, and much more is yet to be found in them; but we have done enough by way of example of the kind of word-by-word examination of your author which is rightly called 'reading,' watching every accent and expression, and putting ourselves always in the author's place, annihilating our own personality, and seeking to enter into his, so as to be able assuredly to say, 'Thus Milton thought,' not 'Thus I thought, in misreading Milton.'"

3. In reading successive poems and prose selections from different authors, strong resemblances in thought or language are frequently detected. It is a thought-provoking process to bring such similar passages to a definite comparison. Even where the same topic is treated differently by two authors, the different or contrasted points of view are suggestive. Calling such familiar passages to mind is in itself a good practice, and it is well to cultivate this mode of turning previous knowledge into use.

To illustrate this point, let us call to mind some familiar passages, touching the winter snow-storm and the fireside comforts, from Whittier, Emerson, and Lowell.

Whittier's description of a snow-storm in "Snow-Bound" is well known: —

>"Unwarmed by any sunset light
>The gray day darkened into night,
>A night made hoary with the swarm
>And whirl-dance of the blinding storm,
>As zigzag wavering to and fro
>Crossed and recrossed the winged snow:
>And ere the early bedtime came
>The white drift piled the window-frame,
>And through the glass the clothes-line posts
>Looked in like tall and sheeted ghosts.
>
>"So all night long the storm roared on:
>The morning broke without a sun;
>In tiny spherule traced with lines
>Of Nature's geometric signs,
>In starry flake and pellicle
>All day the hoary meteor fell;
>And, when the second morning shone,
>We looked upon a world unknown,

> On nothing we could call our own.
> Around the glistening wonder bent
> The blue walls of the firmament,
> No cloud above, no earth below,—
> A universe of sky and snow!
> The old familiar sights of ours
> Took marvellous shapes; strange domes and towers
> Rose up where sty or corn-crib stood,
> Or garden-wall, or belt of wood;
> A smooth white mound the brush-pile showed,
> A fenceless drift what once was road;
> The bridle-post an old man sat
> With loose-flung coat and high cocked hat;
> The well-curb had a Chinese roof;
> And even the long sweep, high aloof,
> In its slant splendor, seemed to tell
> Of Pisa's leaning miracle."

Again the fireside joy is expressed:—

> "Shut in from all the world without,
> We sat the clean-winged hearth about,
> Content to let the north-wind roar
> In baffled rage at pane and door,
> While the red logs before us beat
> The frost-line back with tropic heat;
> And ever, when a louder blast
> Shook beam and rafter as it passed,
> The merrier up its roaring draught
> The great throat of the chimney laughed,
> The house-dog on his paws outspread
> Laid to the fire his drowsy head,
> The cat's dark silhouette on the wall
> A couchant tiger's seemed to fall;
> And, for the winter fireside meet,
> Between the andirons' straddling feet,
> The mug of cider simmered slow,

The apples sputtered in a row,
And, close at hand, the basket stood
With nuts from brown October's wood.

"What matter how the night behaved?
What matter how the north-wind raved?
Blow high, blow low, not all its snow
Could quench our hearth-fire's ruddy glow."

If these passages and others in "Snow-Bound" are familiar to the children in previous study, the reading of Emerson's "The Snow-Storm," might set them to recalling a whole series of pictures from Whittier:—

"Announced by all the trumpets of the sky,
Arrives the snow, and, driving o'er the fields,
Seems nowhere to alight: the whited air
Hides hills and woods, the river, and the heaven,
And veils the farmhouse at the garden's end.
The sled and traveller stopped, the courier's feet
Delayed, all friends shut out, the housemates sit
Around the radiant fireplace, enclosed
In a tumultuous privacy of storm.

"Come see the north wind's masonry.
Out of an unseen quarry evermore,
Furnished with tile, the fierce artificer
Curves his white bastions with projected roof
Round every windward stake, or tree, or door.
Speeding, the myriad-handed, his wild work
So fanciful, so savage, nought cares he
For number or proportion. Mockingly,
On coop or kennel he hangs Parian wreaths;
A swan-like form invests the hidden thorn;
Fills up the farmer's lane from wall to wall,
Maugre the farmer's sighs; and at the gate
A tapering turret overtops the work.
And when his hours are numbered, and the world
Is all his own, retiring, as he were not,

> Leaves, when the sun appears, astonished Art
> To mimic in slow structures, stone by stone,
> Built in an age, the mad wind's night-work,
> The frolic architecture of the snow."

The architecture of the snow can be compared point by point in both authors, in the objects about the farmhouse, while the picture of the snug comforts of the fireplace is in both.

Of a somewhat different, yet closely related, character is the description in the Prelude to Part Second, in the "Vision of Sir Launfal":—

> "Down swept the chill wind from the mountain peak,
>   From the snow five thousand summers old;
> On open wold and hill-top bleak
>   It had gathered all the cold,
> And whirled it like sleet on the wanderer's cheek;
> It carried a shiver everywhere
> From the unleafed boughs and pastures bare;
> The little brook heard it and built a roof
> 'Neath which he could house him, winter-proof;
> All night by the white stars' frosty gleams
> He groined his arches and matched his beams;
> Slender and clear were his crystal spars
> As the lashes of light that trim the stars;
> He sculptured every summer delight
> In his halls and chambers out of sight;
> Sometimes his tinkling waters slipt
> Down through a frost-leaved forest-crypt,
> Long, sparkling aisles of steel-stemmed trees
> Bending to counterfeit a breeze;
> Sometimes the roof no fretwork knew
> But silvery mosses that downward grew;
> Sometimes it was carved in sharp relief
> With quaint arabesques of ice-fern leaf;
> Sometimes it was simply smooth and clear
> For the gladness of heaven to shine through, and here
> He had caught the nodding bulrush-tops

And hung them thickly with diamond drops,
Which crystalled the beams of moon and sun,
And made a star of every one:
No mortal builder's most rare device
Could match this winter-palace of ice;
'Twas as if every image that mirrored lay
In his depths serene through the summer day,
Each flitting shadow of earth and sky,
   Lest the happy model should be lost,
Had been mimicked in fairy masonry
   By the elfin builders of the frost.

"Within the hall are the song and laughter,
   The cheeks of Christmas glow red and jolly,
And sprouting is every corbel and rafter
   With the lightsome green of ivy and holly;
Through the deep gulf of the chimney wide
Wallows the Yule-log's roaring tide;
The broad flame-pennons droop and flap
   And belly and tug as a flag in the wind;
Like a locust shrills the imprisoned sap,
   Hunted to death in its galleries blind;
And swift little troops of silent sparks,
   Now pausing, now scattering away as in fear,
Go threading the soot-forest's tangled darks
   Like herds of startled deer."

   The elfin builders of the frost have raised even more delicate structures than the snow. The descriptive power of the poets in picturing nature's handiwork cannot be better seen than in these passages. It is hardly worth while to suggest the points of resemblance which children will quickly detect in these passages, as the comparison of—

"Through the deep gulf of the chimney wide
Wallows the Yule-log's roaring tide,"

with this,—

"The merrier up its roaring draught.
The great throat of the chimney laughed."

Such passages, suggesting like thoughts in earlier studies, are very frequent and spring up in unexpected quarters.

For example, Emerson, in "Waldeinsamkeit," says:—

"I do not count the hours I spend
  In wandering by the sea;
The forest is my loyal friend,
  Like God it useth me."

Again, in the "Apology," he says:—

"Think me not unkind and rude
  That I walk alone in grove and glen;
I go to the god of the wood
  To fetch his word to men."

And Lowell, in "The Bobolink":—

"As long, long years ago I wandered,
I seem to wander even yet.
The hours the idle schoolboy squandered,
The man would die ere he'd forget.
O hours that frosty eld deemed wasted,
Nodding his gray head toward my books,
I dearer prize the lore I tasted
With you, among the trees and brooks,
Than all that I have gained since then
From learned books or study-withered men."

And Whittier says:—

"Our uncle, innocent of books,
Was rich in lore of fields and brooks,
The ancient teachers never dumb

Of Nature's unhoused lyceum."

It would not be difficult to recall other passages from Bryant, Shakespeare, Byron, and many others, expressing this love of solitude in woods or on the seashore, and the wisdom to be gained from such communion with nature. This active retrospect to gather up kindred thoughts out of previous studies and mingle them with the newer influx of radiant ideas from master minds is a fruitful mode of assimilating and compounding knowledge. It may be advisable at times for the teacher to bring together a few additional passages from still wider sources, expressive of a thought kindred to that worked out in the class. Such study leads to a self-reliant, enthusiastic companionship with the thoughts of great men, and is most profitable.

4. There is a pronounced value in dramatic representation of literary selections. The impersonating of characters gives an intensity and realism to the thought that cannot be effected in any other way. In some cases it is possible to provide a stage and some degree of costuming, to lend more complete realization of the scenes.

In favor of such dramatic efforts it may be said that children, even in the earlier grades, are naturally dramatic, and enjoy greatly both seeing and participating in them. It gives scope to their natural tendency toward action, rather than repose, and proper verbal expression is more easily secured in conjunction with action than without it. In this connection it may be said that acting lends greater freedom and spontaneity to the reading.

Schlegel, in his description of dramatic art, says:—

"Even in a lively oral narration, it is not unusual to introduce persons in conversation with each other, and to give a corresponding variety to the tone and the expression. But the gaps, which these conversations leave in the story, the narrator fills up in his own name with a description of the accompanying circumstances, and other particulars. The dramatic poet must renounce all such expedients; but for this he is richly recompensed in the following invention. He requires each of the characters in his story to be personated by a living individual; that this individual should, in sex, age, and figure, meet as near as may be the prevalent conceptions of his fictitious original, nay, assume his entire personality; that every speech should be delivered in a suitable tone of voice, and accompanied by appropriate action and gesture; and that those external circumstances should be added which are necessary to give the hearers a clear idea of what is going forward. Moreover, these representatives of the creatures of his imagination must appear in the costume belonging to their assumed rank, and to their age and country; partly for the sake of greater resemblance, and partly because, even in dress, there is something characteristic. Lastly, he must see them placed in a locality which, in some degree, resembles that where, according to his fable, the action took place, because this also contributes to the resemblance: he places them, *i.e.*, on a scene. All this brings us to the idea of the theatre. It is evident that the very form of dramatic poetry, that is, the exhibition of an action by dialogue without the aid of narrative, implies the theatre as its necessary complement."

"The invention of dramatic art, and of the theatre, seems a very obvious and natural one. Man has a great disposition to mimicry; when he enters vividly into the situation, sentiments, and passions of others, he involuntarily puts on a resemblance to them in his gestures. Children are perpetually going out of themselves; it is one of their chief amusements to represent those grown people whom they have had an opportunity of observing, or whatever strikes their fancy; and with the happy pliancy of their imagination, they can exhibit all the characteristics of any dignity they may choose to assume, be it that of a father, a schoolmaster, or a king."

In his book, "Imagination and Dramatic Instinct," S. S. Curry says:—

"Since dramatic instinct is so important, the question naturally arises respecting the use of dialogues for its education. There are those who think that all histrionic art is useless; that it is even deleterious to character to assume a part.

"The best answer to this is the study of the little child. The very first means a child adopts to get out of itself, or to realize the great world about it, is by dramatic action and instinct. No child was ever born with any mind at all, that had not some of this instinct; and the more promising the child, the more is it dramatic and imaginative. Dramatic instinct is universal. It is the secret of all success; it is the instinct by which man sees things from different points of view, by which he realizes the ideal in character in contrast to that which is not ideal."

"Professor Monroe was once asked by a clergyman for private lessons. He told him that was impossible. 'Well,' said the minister, 'what can I do then?' 'Go home and read Shakespeare dramatically.' Why was such advice given? Because the struggle to read Shakespeare would get the minister out of himself. The struggle to realize how men of different types of character would speak certain things would make him conscious whether he, himself, spoke naturally. He would, in short, become aware of his mannerisms, of his narrow gamut of emotions, his sameness of point of view; he would be brought into direct contact with the process of his own mind in thinking."

The supreme value of a vivid and versatile imagination in giving full and rich development to the whole mind is now a vital part of our confession of faith. The question is how to cultivate such a resourceful imagination. The literature of the creative imagination is felt to be the chief means, and the dramatic instinct toward interpreting, assimilating and expressing human thought and feeling opens the avenue of growth.

Dr. Curry says:—

"Dramatic instinct should be trained because it is a part of the imagination, because it gives us practical steps toward the development of the imagination, because it is the means of securing discipline and power over feeling. Dramatic instinct should be trained because it is the insight of one mind into another. The man who has killed his dramatic instinct has become unsympathetic, and can never appreciate any one's point of view but his own. Dramatic instinct endows us with broad conceptions of the idiosyncrasies, beliefs, and convictions of men. It trains us to unconscious reasoning, to a deep insight into the motives of man. It is universally felt that one's power to 'other himself' is the measure of the greatness of his personality. All sympathy, all union of ourselves with the ideals and struggles of our race, are traceable to imagination and dramatic instinct."

He further emphasizes the idea that dramatic instinct has two elements—imagination and sympathy. "Imagination affords insight into character; sympathy enables us to identify ourselves with it." "Together they form the chief elements of altruism. They redeem the mind from narrowness and selfishness; they enable the individual to appreciate the point of view, the feelings, motives, and characters of his fellow-men; they open his eyes to read the various languages of human art; they enable him to commune with his kind on a higher plane than that of commonplace facts; they lift him into communion with the art and spirit of every age and nation. Without their development man is excluded from the highest enjoyment, the highest communion with his kind, and from the highest success in every walk of life."

Dramatization is the only means by which we can bring the reading work of the school to its full and natural expression. The action involved in it predisposes the mind to full and natural utterance. The fulfilment of all the dramatic conditions lends an impetus and genuineness to every word that is spoken. It has been often observed that boys and girls whose reading is somewhat expressionless become direct and forcible when taking a part in a dialogue or dramatic action. It would be almost farcical not to put force and meaning into the words when all the other elements of action and realism are present.

Educational progress is everywhere exerting a distinct pressure at those points where greater realism, deeper absorption in actualities, is possible. This is the significance of outdoor excursions, of experiments, laboratories, and object work in nature study. In geography and history it is the purpose of pictures, vivid descriptions, biographical stories, and the accounts of eye-witnesses and real travellers, etc.

In literature we possess, embodied in striking concrete personalities, many of the most forcible ideas that men have conceived and dealt with in the history of the world. It is very desirable that children should become themselves the vehicles for the expression of these ideas. The school is the place where children should become the embodiment of ideas. It would be a grand and not impractical scheme of education to propose to make the school a place where each child, in a well-chosen succession, should be allowed to impersonate and become the embodiment of the constructive ideas of our civilization.

We reason much concerning the educative value of carpentry, of the various forms of manual skill in wood and iron, of weaving, gardening, and cooking, of the work of shoemaker, basket-maker, and potter, and of the educative value of these constructive activities; for the purposes of universal education, is it not of equal importance that children become skilled in the histrionic art, in the apt interpretation and expression of good manners, in that deeper social insight and versatile tact which are the constructive elements in conduct? Or, putting it in a more obvious form, is it any more important for a person to know how to construct a bookcase or even a steam-engine, than to shape his speech or conduct skilfully in meeting a board of education or a business manager.

It is not the purpose of the school to educate players or public readers, any more than to train carpenters or machinists. But the reading exercises in school should culminate in the ability to sympathetically interpret a considerable variety of human life and character as presented in our best literature. Modern educators, however, are not satisfied, in any important study, with theoretical knowledge derived from books. They demand that knowledge shall pass over into some sort of practice and use. Reading passes naturally and without a break from the interpretation of life to its embodiment in conduct. In this important respect it is the most practical of all studies. Its subject matter, derived from literature, consists largely of an interesting variety of typical and artistically beautiful character delineations from the hands of the supreme master of this art. Dramatic representation is the last and indispensable step in the art of reading; and the interest that naturally attaches to it, from early childhood up through all the stages of growth, removes one chief obstacle to its introduction.

Keeping in mind that wisdom, skill, and versatility in conduct are the natural and appropriate outcome of successful dramatic representation, it is not at all extravagant to say that the average child will have far more use for this result, both now and in all the vicissitudes of later life, than for skill in carpentry, or ironwork, or weaving, etc.

Nor have we any disposition to detract from the value usually attributed to manual training in its various forms by its advocates.

It is not uncommon for teachers generally to employ the dialogue form when the selection admits of it, and to assign the parts to different children. Our purpose, however, in the fuller discussion and emphasis of the dramatic element is to suggest a more liberal employment of dramatic selections, and to provide for a much fuller dramatic representation, using simple, inexpensive costumes and stage surroundings where possible.

When we examine in detail the number of dramatic selections in a set of readers, or among the masterpieces sometimes read in the classes below the high school, we shall find a number of purely dramatic works. "The Merchant of Venice" and "Julius Cæsar" are well adapted to seventh and eighth grades, and there are many selections in which the dialogue is an important feature, as in "The Cricket on the Hearth," "King of the Golden River," "Tanglewood Tales," "Lady of the Lake," "Marmion," "Pilgrim's Progress," "Grandfather's Chair," and many others.

"The Courtship of Miles Standish" has been published in a form specially adapted for school exhibitions by Houghton, Mifflin, & Co. Longfellow's "Giles Corey of the Salem Farms," in the "Riverside Series," is a drama well suited to sixth grade. The story of "William Tell," derived from Schiller's drama, is adapted to sixth and possibly to fifth grade.

Some of the ballads are cast in the form of the dialogue, and can be easily treated so in the school, as "Proud Lady Margaret," "Robin Hood and the Widow's Sons," "King John and the Abbot of Canterbury," and many others. The Robin Hood stories are full of dialogue and could be easily dramatized, and so with "Uncle Tom's Cabin," and others.

An examination of our literature from this point of view will discover a strong dramatic element in a large portion of it, and the cultivation of this spirit will qualify the children for a better appreciation of many of the great works.

5. Treatment of the "Odyssey."

The "Odyssey" is probably as well known as any masterpiece in the world's literature. For the sake of illustration, therefore, we will enter upon a brief discussion of the mode of handling it as a unit in the school.

There are abundant sources in English from which the teacher can get an adequate knowledge of this great poem without using the original Greek. A few of the leading books which the teacher may consult are as follows: "The Story of Ulysses" (Cook). A very simple, abbreviated narrative of

Ulysses' wanderings, sometimes used as a reading book in fourth or fifth grade. (Public School Publishing Co.)—"Lamb's Adventures of Ulysses." A pleasing prose rendering of the chief incidents of the story, more difficult than the preceding. Sometimes used as a reader. (Ginn & Co.)—"Church's Stories of the Old World," in which "The Adventures of Ulysses" forms a chapter. A good short treatment of the story in simple language. (Ginn & Co.)—"Ulysses among the Phæacians," consisting of selections from five books of the "Odyssey" as translated into verse by Bryant. This seems well adapted for use as a reading-book in fourth or fifth grade, and will be discussed more fully as such. (Houghton, Mifflin, & Co.)—"The Odyssey of Homer" by Palmer, is an excellent prose-poetic rendering of the whole poem, and is of great service to the teacher. (Houghton, Mifflin, & Co.)—Another excellent prose translation, by Butcher and Lang, has been much used. (The Macmillan Co.)—Bryant's "Homer's 'Odyssey,'" a complete poetic rendering of the whole twenty-four books of the poem, is probably the best basis for school reference and study of the poem.—"National Epics," by Rabb, has a good narrative and introduction for the "Odyssey," and a list of critical references. (A. C. McClurg & Co.)—"Art and Humanity in Homer," by Lawton, has an interesting discussion of the "Odyssey." Other famous translations of the whole "Odyssey" were made by Alexander Pope, William Cowper, George Chapman, and others.

It is not unusual in schools for teachers to give children of the third or fourth grade an oral introduction to the whole story in a series of lessons. This requires skill in presenting and discussing the episodes, and should be attended by good oral reproductions by the children. Such oral work should be done in distinct lessons apart from the regular reading. Later, in fourth or fifth grade, the story is sometimes read in class from one of the simple prose narratives of Miss Cook, or Lamb, or Church. In the fifth or sixth grade, "Ulysses among the Phæacians" forms an interesting reading-book, with which to acquaint the children more fully with the poetic beauty and descriptive detail of the original, so far as it can be secured in English. In connection with such reading it may be interesting to choose from Bryant's complete translation other selected parts of the story, and encourage the children to read them, if books from the library or homes can be provided.

We may dwell for a moment upon those qualities of Homer's story which have commanded the admiration of the great poets in different ages and countries. The peculiar poetic charm and power of the original Greek are probably untranslatable, although several eminent poets have attempted it. But we have at least both prose and verse renderings of it that are beautiful and poetic.

Some of the critics have said that the whole poem is a perfect unit in thought,—much more so than the "Iliad,"—centring in the person of Ulysses. His wanderings and his final return constitute the thread of the narrative. In the main it is a story of peace, with descriptions of cities, islands, palaces, strange lands, and peaceful arts and manners. After their return from Troy we meet Nestor and Menelaus, dwelling happily in their palaces and surrounded with home comforts. Ulysses, himself, the great sufferer, is tossed about the world, or held captive on sea-girt, far-away islands. He passes through a series of wonderful adventures, keeping his alertness and balance of mind so completely that his name has become a synonym in all lands for shrewdness and far-seeing wisdom. And it is not only a wise perception, but a self-control in the midst of old and new temptations which is most remarkable. This over-mastering shrewdness or calculation even overdoes itself and becomes amusing, when he tries, for example, to deceive his guardian goddess as to who he is. The descriptions of women and of domestic life are famous and delightful. The constancy of Penelope, her industry and shrewdness in outwitting the suitors, have given her a supreme place among the women of story. The descriptions of peaceful manners and customs, of public games, of feasting and music, of palace halls and ornament, are among the great literary pictures of the world.

The particular adventures through which Ulysses passed with Circe, with the Sirens, with Polyphemus, with Eolus, with the lotus-eaters, and others, are plainly suggestive of the dangers which threaten the thoughtless minded, those who plunge headlong into danger without forethought. Ulysses does not give way to folly or passion, is bold and skilful in danger, and persevering to the last extreme.

In the treatment of the "Odyssey," the teacher will need a general knowledge of Greek mythology, which can be easily derived from "Greek Gods, Heroes, and Men" (Scott, Foresman, & Co.), and from several other of the reference books. Some study of Greek architecture, sculpture, and modes of life will be instructive and helpful, as given in Smith's "History of Greece" and other histories. Pictures of Greek temples and ruins, sculpture, and palaces will be pleasing and attractive to children. (See Lübke's "History of Art," Vol. I, Dodd, Mead, & Co.) Some of the children's books also contain good pictures.

A good map, indicating the supposed wanderings of Ulysses in the Mediterranean, is given in several of the books, *e.g.* in Palmer's "Odyssey," and fixes many of the most interesting events of the story. The teacher should not overlook the geography of the story and its relation to this and later studies in history, literature, and geography.

In using "Ulysses among the Phæacians" as a reader in fourth or fifth grade, the first unit of study is the voyage of Ulysses on his raft, from the time of leaving Calypso till he is wrecked by the storm and driven upon the island of Scheria, the home of the Phæacians. We will suggest a few points in the treatment. The supposed places and the route of the voyage can be traced on the map. Let the teacher sketch it on the board in assigning the lesson. Suggest that the children locate in the sky the stars and constellations by which Ulysses is to direct his course. The story of the construction of the raft on which Ulysses is to make this journey, just preceding this part of the story, could be read to the class by the teacher, as it is not contained in these extracts. In length of time how does this voyage compare with a voyage across the Atlantic to-day? Why is it said, in line 329, that the Great Bear "alone dips not into the waters of the deep"?

From previous studies, the children may be able to tell of Ulysses' stay upon the island with Calypso. What may the children know of Neptune? Why is he angered with Ulysses? A picture of Neptune with the trident is in place. Explain the expression "while from above the night fell suddenly." Was Ulysses justified in saying, "Now must I die a miserable death"? In spite of the desperate storm, in what ways does Ulysses struggle to save his life? How do the gods assist him? In what way does this experience of Ulysses remind us of Robinson Crusoe's shipwreck and escape?

With how many men had Ulysses started on his way to Troy? Now he alone escapes after great suffering and hopeless buffetings. In what way during this voyage and shipwreck did Ulysses display his accustomed shrewdness and foresight? After landing, what dangers did he still fear?

The nearly three hundred lines of Book V, which give this account of Ulysses' voyage and shipwreck, will require several lessons, and the above questions are but a few of those raised in its reading and discussion. When Neptune, Ulysses, or Ino speak, let the speaker be impersonated so as to give greater force and reality. In the next book (VI), there is more of dialogue and better opportunity for variety of manner and voice.

It would be tedious to enter into further detail suggesting questions. But we may believe that a spirited treatment of this part of the story of Ulysses in reading lessons, including his stay and treatment among the Phæacians, will give the children much appreciation of the beauty and power of this old story. By means of occasional readings of other selected parts of the "Odyssey," from Bryant or Palmer, some of the most striking pictures in the story of his wanderings can be presented. Even the children may find time for some of this additional, outside reading. In any event the story of Ulysses, as a piece of great literature, can thus be brought home to the understandings and hearts of children, and will constitute henceforward a part of that rich furniture of the mind which we call culture.

SUMMARY OF SIGNIFICANT POINTS IN READING

1. The teacher's effort is first directed to a vivid interpretation of the author's thought and feeling, and later to an expressive rendering of the thought.

2. Every exertion should be made to lead the children to an absorbed and interested attention in the selections.

3. The author's leading motive in the whole selection should be firmly grasped by the teacher. By centring all discussion toward this motive, unnecessary digressions will be avoided.

4. The teacher will hardly teach well unless he has saturated himself with the spirit of the selection, and enjoys it. To this end he needs not only to study the selection, but also the historical, geographical, biographical, and other side-lights.

5. The teacher needs great freedom and versatility in the use of his materials. Warmth, animation, and freedom of manner are necessary.

6. Children often do not know how to study a reading lesson. In the assignment and in the way of handling the lesson they should be taught how to get at it, how to understand and enjoy it.

7. In the assignment of the lesson the thought of the piece should be opened up in an interesting way, and such difficulties as children are not likely to grapple with and master for themselves pointed out and approached. Difficult words need to be pronounced and hard passages explained.

8. The assignment should be unmistakably clear and definite, so as to insure a good seat study.

9. The seat study should be chiefly on parts already discussed in class.

10. During the recitation proper, strong class attention by all the members of the class is a first necessity. Much knowledge, alertness, and skill are necessary to secure this. One must keep all the members of the class in the eye constantly, and distribute the questions and work among them promptly and judiciously, so as to secure concentrated effort.

11. The teacher can often judge a recitation better without looking at the book while the class is reading.

12. Skill in questioning is very useful in reading lessons.

(*a*) Questions to arouse the thought should appeal to the experience of children.

(*b*) Questions to bring out the meaning of words or passages, or to expose errors or to develop thought, should be clear and specific, not long and ambiguous.

13. Let the teacher be satisfied with reasonable answers, and not insist on the precise verbal form present to his own mind.

14. The teacher needs to awaken strongly the imagination in picturing scenes, in interpreting poetic images and figures, and in impersonating characters. The picture-forming power is stimulated by apt questions, by suggestion of the teacher, by interpretation, by appeal to experience, by dramatic action.

15. The use of the dialogue and dramatic representation is among the best means of awakening interest and producing freedom and self-forgetfulness.

16. The pupil should give his own interpretation, subject to correction, and interpret parts in relation to the whole.

17. Without too much loss of time children should learn to help themselves in overcoming difficulties in solving problems.

18. Sometimes it is well for children to come prepared to ask definite questions on parts they do not understand.

19. The tendency to more independent and mature thinking is encouraged by comparing similar ideas, figures of speech, and language in different poems and from different authors.

20. There should be much effective reading and not much mere oral reproduction. The paraphrase may be used at times to give the pupil a larger view of the content of the piece.

21. Let the pupil reading feel responsible for giving to the class the content of the printed page. Often it is best to face the class.

22. The teacher should occasionally read a passage in the best style for the pupils, not for direct imitation, but to suggest the higher ideals and spirit of good reading. A high standard is thus set up.

23. Children should be encouraged to learn by heart the passages they like. In the midst of the recitation it is well occasionally to memorize a passage.

24. The teacher must drill himself in clear-cut enunciation of short vowels, final consonants, and pure vowel sounds. Cultivate also a quick ear for accurate enunciation in the pupils and for pleasing tones. Frequent drill exercise, singly and in concert, is necessary.

25. Use ingenuity by indirect methods to overcome nasality, stuttering, nervously rapid reading, slovenly and careless expression, monotone, and singsong.

26. By means of physical training, deep breathing, vigorous thought work, encourage to self-reliant manner and good physical position.

27. Give variety to each lesson; avoid monotony and humdrum.

28. Each lesson should emphasize a particular aim, determined by the nature of the selection or by the previous bad habits and faults of the children in reading. It is impossible to give proper emphasis to all things in each lesson, and indefiniteness and monotony are the result.

CHAPTER VI

THE VALUE OF CLASSICS TO THE TEACHER

In discussing the value and fruitfulness of this field of study to children, it is impossible to forbear the suggestion of its scope and significance for teachers. If the masters of song and expression are able to work so strongly upon the immature minds of children, how much deeper the influence upon the mature and thoughtful minds of teachable teachers! They above all others should have dispositions receptive of the best educational influences. The duties and experiences of their daily work predispose them toward an earnest and teachable spirit. In very many cases, therefore, their minds are wide open to the reception of the best. And how deep and wide and many-sided is this enfranchisement of the soul through literature!

It is a gateway to history; not, however, that castaway shell which our text-books, in the form of a dull recital of facts, call history; but its heart and soul, the living, breathing men and women, the source and incentive of great movements and struggles toward the light. Literature does not make the study of history superfluous, but it puts a purpose into history which lies deeper than the facts, it sifts out the wheat from the chaff, casts aside the superficial and accidental, and gets down into the deep current of events where living causes are at work.

The "Courtship of Miles Standish," for example, is deeper and stronger than history because it idealizes the stern and rigid qualities of the Puritan, while John Alden and Priscilla touch a deeper universal sympathy, and body forth in forms of beauty that pulsing human love which antedates the Puritan and underlies all forms of religion and society.

Illustrative cases have been given in sufficient abundance to show that literature, among other things, has a strong political side. It grasps with a master hand those questions which involve true patriotism. It exalts them into ideals, and fires the hearts of the people to devotion and sacrifice for their fulfilment.

Burke's "Oration on the American War" is, to one who has studied American history, an astonishing confirmation of how righteous and far-sighted were the principles for which Samuel Adams and the other patriots struggled at the opening of the Revolution. Webster's speech at Bunker Hill is a graphic and fervent retrospect on the past of a great struggle, and a prophetic view of the swelling tide of individual, social, and national well-being.

If the teacher is to interpret history to school children, he must learn to grasp what is essential and vital; he must be able to discriminate between those events which are trivial and those of lasting concern. The study of our best American literature will reveal to him this distinction, and make him a keen and comprehensive critic of political affairs.

Barnett, in his "Common Sense in Education and Teaching" (p. 170), says:—

"In the second place, literature provides us with historical landmarks. We cannot be said to understand the general 'history' of a particular time unless we know something of the thought that stirred its most subtle thinkers, and interpreted and made articulate the spirit of the times in which they lived. The most notable facts in the history of the times of Edward III, of Elizabeth, and of Victoria are that Chaucer and Shakespeare and Tennyson and their contemporaries lived and wrote. Political history, social history, economic history, even ecclesiastical history, are all reflected, illustrated, and interpreted by what we find in the great works of contemporary literature."

Charles Kingsley, in his "Literary and General Essays" (p. 249), holds a like opinion:—

"I said that the ages of history were analogous to the ages of man, and that each age of literature was the truest picture of the history of its day, and for this very reason English literature is the best, perhaps the only, teacher of English history, to women especially. For it seems to me that it is principally by the help of such an extended literary course that we can cultivate a just and enlarged taste which will connect education with the deepest feelings of the heart."

Literature is also a mirror that reflects many sides of social life and usage. There is no part of a teacher's education that is so vital to his practical success as social culture. John Locke's "Thoughts on Education" are, in the main, an inquiry into the methods and means by which an English gentleman can be formed. The aim of the tutor who has this difficult task is not chiefly to give learning, to fill the mind with information, to develop mentality, but to train the practical judgment in harmony with gentlemanly conduct. The tutor, himself a scholar, is to know the world, its ins and outs, its varieties of social distinction and usage, its snares and pitfalls, its wise men and fools. The child is to learn to look the world in the face and understand it, to know himself and to be master of himself and of his conduct, to appreciate other people in their moods and characters, and to adapt himself prudently and with tact to the practical needs. The gentleman whom Locke sets up as his ideal is not a fashion-plate figure, not a drawing-room gallant, but a clear-headed man who understands other people and himself, and has been led by insensible degrees to so shape his habitual conduct as most wisely to answer his needs in the real world. Emerson, with all his lofty idealism and unconventionalism, has an ideal of education nearly akin to that of Locke. This social ideal of Locke and Emerson is one that American teachers can well afford to ponder. As a nation, we have been accustomed to think that a certain amount of roughness and boorishness was necessary as a veil to cover the strongest manly qualities. Smoothness and tact and polish, however successful they may be in real life, are, theoretically at least, at a discount. The Adamses, Jefferson, Jackson, Lincoln, Thoreau, were men who did violence in a good many ways to social usages, and we may admire their faults overmuch.

To the teacher who stands in the presence of thirty or fifty distinct species of incipient men and women, social insight and culture, the ability to appreciate each in his individual traits, his strength or weakness, are a prime essential to good educative work.

Now, there are two avenues through which social culture is attainable,—contact with men and women in the social environment which envelops us all, and literature. Literature is, first of all, a hundred-sided revelation of human conduct as springing from motive. Irving, Hawthorne, Longfellow, Holmes, and Lowell are revealers of humanity. Still more so are Dickens and Eliot and Shakespeare and Goethe. To study these authors is not simply to enjoy the graphic power of an artist, but to look into the lives of so many varieties of men and women. They lay bare the heart and its inward promptings. Our appreciation for many forms of life under widely differing conditions is awakened. We come in touch with those typical varieties of men and women whom we shall daily meet if we will but notice. It broadens one's perceptions and sympathies, it reveals the many-sidedness of human life. It suggests to a teacher that the forty varieties of humanity in her schoolroom are not after one pattern, nor to be manipulated according to a single device.

The social life that surrounds each one of us is small and limited. Our intimate companionships are few, and we can see deeply into the inner life of but a small portion even of those about us. The deeper life of thought and feeling is largely covered up with conventionalities and externalities. But in the works of the best novelists, dramatists, and poets, we may look abroad into the whole world of time and place, upon an infinite variety of social conditions, and we are permitted to see directly into the inner thought and motive, the very soul of the actors. Yet fidelity to human nature and real life is claimed to be the peculiar merit of these great writers. By the common consent of critics, Shakespeare is the prince of character delineators. Schlegel says of him:—

"Shakespeare's knowledge of mankind has become proverbial; in this his superiority is so great that he has justly been called the master of the human heart. A readiness to remark the mind's fainter and involuntary utterances, and the power to express with certainty the meaning of these signs, as determined by experience and reflection, constitute 'the observer of men.'"

"After all, a man acts so because he is so. And what each man is, that Shakespeare reveals to us most immediately; he demands and obtains our belief, even for what is singular and deviates from the ordinary course of nature. Never perhaps was there so comprehensive a talent for characterization as Shakespeare. It not only grasps every diversity of rank, age, and sex, down to the lispings of infancy; not only do the king and the beggar, the hero and the pickpocket, the sage and the idiot, speak and act with equal truthfulness; not only does he transport himself to distant ages and foreign nations, and portray with the greatest accuracy (a few apparent violations of costume excepted) the spirit of the ancient Romans, of the French in the wars with the English, of the English themselves during a great part of their history, of the Southern Europeans (in the serious part of many comedies), the cultivated society of the day, and the rude barbarism of a Norman foretime; his human characters have not only such depth and individuality that they do not admit of being classed under common names, and are inexhaustible even in conception,—no, this Prometheus not merely forms men, he opens the gates of the magical world of spirits."

What is true of Shakespeare in a preëminent degree is true to a marked extent of all the great novelists and poets.

The teacher needs to possess great versatility and tact in social situations. A quick insight, social ease, freedom, and self-possession are of the first importance to him. The power of sympathy, of appreciation for others' feelings and difficulties, is wholly dependent upon such social cultivation. Otherwise the teacher will be rude, even uncouth and boorish in manner, producing friction and ill-will where tact and gentleness would bring sympathy and confidence. Many people absorb this refinement of thought and manner from the social circles with which they mingle, and it is, of course, a smiling fortune that has placed a teacher's early life in a happy and cultured atmosphere, where the social sympathies and graces are absorbed almost unconsciously. But even where the earlier conditions have been less favorable, the opportunity for rapid social development and culture is most promising. The numberless cases in our country in which young people, by the strength of their energetic purpose and desire for improvement, have raised themselves not only to superior knowledge and scholarship, but also to that far greater refinement of social life and manner which we call true culture,—the numberless instances of this sort are a surprising indication of the power of education. Literature has been a potent agent in this direction. It emancipates, it sets free, the spirit of man. It lifts him above what is sordid and material, and gives him those true standards of worth with which to measure all things. It contains within itself the refining elements, the æsthetic and ethical ideals, and, best of all, it portrays human life in all its thought, feeling, and passion with such intensity and realistic fidelity that its teaching power is unparalleled.

This potentiality of the better literature to produce such noble results in the higher range of culture is dependent upon conditions. No one will understand literature who does not study and understand ordinary life as it surrounds him; who does not constantly draw upon his own experience in interpreting the characters portrayed in books. No stupid or unobservant person will be made wise through books, be they never so choice. Even the student who works laboriously at his text-books, but has no eye nor care for the people or doings about him, is getting only the mechanical side of education, and is losing the better part. He who will draw riches out of books must put his intellect and sympathy, his whole enthusiastic better self, into them.

The indwelling virtue of great books is that they demand this intense awakening, this complete absorption of the whole self. The mind of a child and of a man or woman has to stretch itself to the utmost limit to take in the message of a great writer. One feels the old barriers giving way and the mind expanding to the conception of larger things. Speaking of the ancient drama at Athens, Shelley says, "The imagination is enlarged by a sympathy with pains and passions so mighty that they distend in their conception the capacity of that by which they are conceived."

Those who have received into the inner self the expansive energy of noble thought and social culture, are the better qualified, from the rich variety of the inner life, to act effectively upon the complex conditions and forces of the outer world. The teacher whose inner life is teeming with these rich sympathies and potent ideals will react with greater prudence and tact upon the kaleidoscopic conditions of a school.

Practical social life and literature are not distinct modes of culture. They are one, they interact upon each other in scores of ways. Give a teacher social opportunities, give him the best of our literature, let these two work their full influence upon him,—then, if he cannot become a teacher, it is a hopeless case. Let him go to the shop, to the farm, to the legislature; there is no place for him in the schoolroom.

Literature is also a sharp and caustic critic of his own follies or foibles, to one who can reflect. It has a multitude of surprises by which we are able, as Burns wished,—

"To see oursels as ithers see us."

Even the schoolmaster finds an occasional apt description of himself in literature which it is often interesting and entertaining for him to ponder. One of the most familiar is that of Goldsmith in "The Deserted Village":—

"Beside yon straggling fence that skirts the way
With blossomed furze unprofitably gay,
There, in his noisy mansion, skill'd to rule,
The village master taught his little school.
A man severe he was, and stern to view;
I knew him well, and every truant knew:
Well had the boding tremblers learn'd to trace
The day's disasters in his morning face;
Full well they laugh'd, with counterfeited glee,
At all his jokes, for many a joke had he;
Full well the busy whisper, circling round,
Convey'd the dismal tidings when he frown'd.
Yet he was kind, or, if severe in aught,
The love he bore to learning was in fault.
The village all declar'd how much he knew;
'Twas certain he could write, and cipher too;
Lands he could measure, terms and tides presage,
And even the story ran that he could gauge;
In arguing, too, the parson own'd his skill,
For even though vanquish'd he could argue still;
While words of learned length and thundering sound
Amaz'd the gazing rustics ranged around;
And still they gaz'd, and still the wonder grew
That one small head could carry all he knew."

A like entertainment and suggestion of what the schoolmaster may be, as seen by others, are furnished by Irving's Ichabod Crane. William Shenstone's description of the schoolmistress and the school near two hundred years ago in his native village, is very diverting. Charles Dickens's description of schools and schoolmasters is important in the history of

England, and, like his portrayals of child life generally, of deep pedagogical worth to teachers.

In his book, "The Schoolmaster in Literature," Mr. Skinner has done a real service to the teaching world in bringing together, into a convenient compilation from many sources, the literature bearing directly upon the schoolmaster. Even the comic representations and caricatures are valuable in calling attention to common foibles and mannerisms, to say nothing of the more serious faults of teachers.

It is in literature, also, and in those lives and scenes from history which literary artists have worked up, that the teacher can best develop his own moral ideals and strengthen the groundwork of his own moral character. The stream will not rise above its source, and a teacher's moral influence in a school will not reach above the inspirations from high sources which he himself has felt. Those teachers who have devoted themselves solely to the mastery of the texts they teach, who have read little from our best writers, are drawing upon a slender capital of moral resource. Not even if home influences have laid a sound basis of moral habits are these sufficient reserves for the exigencies of teaching. The moral nature of the teacher needs constant stimulus to upward growing, and the children need examples, ideal illustrations, life and blood impersonations of the virtues; and literature is the chief and only safe reservoir from which to draw them.

We have already discussed the moral value of the right books for children. The lessons of the great works are so profound in this respect that they offer a still wider range of study to the teacher. Even the foremost thinkers and philosophers have found therein an inexhaustible source of truth and wisdom.

In the Foreword to his "Great Books as Life Teachers," Newell Dwight Hillis says, "For some reason our generation has closed its text-books on ethics and morals, and opened the great poems, essays, and novels." This is a remarkable statement and is the key-note to a silent but sweeping change in education. He adds, "Doubtless for thoughtful persons this fact argues, not a decline of interest in the fundamental principles of right living, but a desire to study these principles as they are made flesh and embodied in living persons." Again, "It seems important to remember that the great novelists are consciously or unconsciously teachers of morals, while the most fascinating essays and poems are essentially books of aspiration and spiritual culture."

It is suggestive to note that this fundamental text is worked out in his book by chapters on Ruskin's "Seven Lamps of Architecture," George Eliot's "Romola," Hawthorne's "Scarlet Letter," Victor Hugo's "Les Miserables," Tennyson's "Idylls of the King," and Browning's "Saul." This suggests a fruitful line of studies for every teacher.

Among modern essayists, Emerson, Carlyle, Ruskin, and Matthew Arnold stand preëminent, and they are already well established among the mightiest teachers of our age, and it may be, of many to come. Sure it is that teachers could not do better than put themselves within earshot of these resonant voices. Their heart-strings will vibrate and their intellects will be stretched to a full tension, not simply by the music, but by the truth which surges up and bursts into utterance. It is scarcely a figure of speech to say that the lightning flashes across their pages. The stinging rebuke of wrong, the noble ideals of righteousness, place them among the prophets whose tongues have been touched with fire from the altar.

Besides the historical, social, and moral tuition for teachers in literature, there are several other important culture effects in it. The deepest religious incentives are touched, nature in her myriad phases is observed with the eye of the poet and scientist, and the æsthetic side of poetry and rhythmic prose, its charm and graces of style, its music and eloquence, work their influence upon the reader. Literature is a harp of many strings, and happy is that teacher who has learned to detect its tones and overtones, who has listened with pleasure to its varied raptures, and has felt that expansion of soul which it produces.

Literature, in the sense in which we have been using it, has been called the literature of power, the literature of the spirit. That is, it has generative, spiritual life. It is not simple knowledge, it is knowledge energized, charged with potency. It is knowledge into which the poet has breathed the breath of life. The difference between bare knowledge and the literature of power is like the difference between a perfect statue in stone and a living, pulsing, human form.

One of the virtues of literature, therefore, is the mental stimulus, the joy, the awakening, the intensity of thought it spontaneously calls forth. Textbooks are usually a bore, but literature is a natural resource even in hours of weariness. Who would dream of enlivening leisure hours or vacation rest with text-books of grammar, or arithmetic, or history, or science? But the poet soothes with music, solemn or gay, according to our choice. If we go to the woods or lakes to escape our friends, we take one of the masters of song with us. After a day of toil and weariness, we can turn to "Evangeline," or "Lady of the Lake," or the "Vision of Sir Launfal," and soon we are listening to—

"The murmuring pines and the hemlocks,"

or the echo of the hunter's horn,—

"The deep-mouthed bloodhound's heavy bay
Resounded up the rocky way,
And faint, from farther distance borne,
Were heard the clanging hoof and horn."

At a time when we are not fit for the irksome and perfunctory preparation of text-book lessons, we are still capable of receiving abundant entertainment or hearty inspiration from Warner's "How I killed a Bear," or Tennyson's "Enoch Arden," or "Sleepy Hollow." Literature is recreation in its double sense. It gives rest and relief, and it builds up.

Teachers should shake themselves free from the conviction that severe disciplinary studies are the best part of education. They have their well-merited place. But there are higher spiritual fountains from which to draw. Read the lives of Scott, Macaulay, Irving, Hawthorne, and Emerson, and discover that the things we do with the greatest inward spontaneity and pleasure and ease are often the best.

Literature, both in prose and verse, is what the teacher needs, because our best authors are our best teachers in their method of handling their subjects. They know how to find access to the reader's mind by making their ideas attractive, interesting, and beautiful. They seem to know how to sharpen the edge of truth to render it more keen and incisive. They drive truth deeper, so that it remains embedded in the life and thought. Let a poet clothe an idea with strength and wing it with fancy, and it will find its way straight to the heart. First of all, nearly all our classic writers, especially those we use in the grades, handle their subjects from the concrete, graphic, picturesque side. They not only illustrate abundantly from nature and real things in life; they nearly always individualize and personify their ideas. Virtue to a poet is nothing unless it is impersonated. A true poet is never abstract or dry or formal in his treatment of a subject. It is natural for a literary artist, whether in verse or prose, to create pictures, to put all his ideas into life forms and bring them close to the real ones in nature. Homer's idea of wisdom is Minerva, war is Mars, strength is Ajax, skill and prudence are Ulysses, faithfulness is Penelope. Dickens does not talk about schoolmasters in general, but of Squeers. Shakespeare's idea of jealousy is not a definition, not a formula, but Othello. Those books which have enthralled the world, like "Robinson Crusoe," "Pilgrim's Progress," "Gulliver's Travels," "Arabian Nights," "Evangeline," "Ivanhoe," "Merchant of Venice,"—they deal with no form of classified or generalized knowledge; they give us no definitions, they are scenes from real life. They stand among realities, and their roots are down in the soil of things. They are persons hemmed in by the close environment of facts.

This realism, this objectifying of thought, this living form of knowledge, is characteristic of all great writers in prose or verse. The novelist, the romancer, the poet, the orator, and even the essayist, will always put the breath of reality into his work by an infusion of concreteness, of graphic personification. The poet's fancy, building out of the abundant materials of sense-experience, is what gives color and warmth to all his thoughts. Strong writers make incessant use of figures of speech. Their thought must clothe itself with the whole panoply of imagery and graphic representation in order to be efficient in the warfare for truth.

What a lesson for the teacher! What models upon which to develop his style of thinking! If the teaching profession and its work could be weighed in the balance, the scale would fall on the side of the abstract with a heavy thud. Not that object lessons will save us. They only parody the truth. For the object lesson as a separate thing we have no use at all. But to ground every idea and every study in realism, to pass up steadily through real objects and experience to a perception of truths which have wide application, to science—this is the true philosophy of teaching.

The classic writers lead us even one grand step beyond realism. The fancy builds better than the cold reason. It adorns and ennobles thought till it becomes full-fledged for the flight toward the ideal.

As the poet, standing by the sea-shore, ponders the life that has been in the now empty shell washed up from the deep, his fancy discovers in the shell a resemblance to human life and destiny, and he cries:—

> "Build thee more stately mansions, O my soul,
> As the swift seasons roll!
> Leave thy low-vaulted past!
> Let each new temple, nobler than the last,
> Shut thee from heaven with a dome more vast,
> Till thou at length art free,
> Leaving thine outgrown shell by life's unresting sea!"

Is it possible that one could fall under the sway of the poets and artists, appropriate their images and fruitful style of thought, be wrought upon by their fancies, and still remain dull and lifeless and prosaic in the classroom? No wonder that true literature has been called the literature of power, as distinguished from the literature of knowledge (supplementary readers, pure science, information books, etc.). The lives and works of our best writers contain an expansive spiritual energy, which, working into the mind of a teacher, breaks the shell of mechanism and formality. The artist gives bright tints and colors to ideas which would otherwise be faded and bleached.

The study of the best literature adapted to children in each age is a fruitful form of psychology and child study. The series of books selected for the different grades is supposed to be adapted to the children at each period. The books which suit the temper and taste of children in primary grades are peculiar in quality, and fit those pupils better than older ones. In intermediate classes the boyhood spirit, which delights in myth, physical deeds of prowess, etc., shows itself, and many of the stories, ballads, and longer poems breathe this spirit. In grammar grades the expanding, maturing minds of children leap forward to the appreciation of more complex and extended forms of literature which deal with some of the great problems of life more seriously, as "Snow-Bound," "Evangeline," "Roger de Coverley," "Merchant of Venice," etc.

Any poem or story which is suited to pupils of the common school may generally be used in several grades. Hawthorne's "Wonder Book," for instance, may be used anywhere from the third to the eighth grade by a skilful teacher. But for us the important question is, to what age of children is it best adapted? Where does its style of thought best fit the temper of the children? The eighth grade may read it and get pleasure and good from it, but it does not come up to the full measure of their needs. Children of the third grade cannot master it with sufficient ease, but in the latter part of the fourth or first part of the fifth grade it seems to exactly suit the wants, that is, the spiritual wants, of the children. It will vary, of course, in different schools and classes. Now, it is a problem for our serious consideration to determine what stories to use and just where each belongs, within reasonable limits. Let us inquire where the best culture effect can be realized from each book used, where it is calculated to work its best and strongest influence. To accomplish this result it is necessary to study equally the temper of the children and the quality of the books, to seek the proper food for the growing mind at its different stages. This is not chiefly a matter of simplicity or complexity of language. Our readers are largely graded by the difficulty of language. But literature should be distributed through the school grades according to its power to arouse thought and interest. Language will have to be regarded, but as secondary. Look first to the thought material which is to engage children's minds, and then force the language into subservice to that end. The final test to determine the place of a selection in the school course must be the experiment of the class-room. We may exercise our best judgment beforehand, and later find that a classic belongs one or two grades higher or lower than we thought.

We really need some comprehensive principle upon which to make the selection of materials as adapted to the nature (psychology) of children. The theory of the culture epochs of race history as parallel to child development offers at least a suggestion. A few of the great periods of history seem to correspond fairly well to certain epochs of child growth. The age of folk-lore and the fairy tale is often called the childhood of the race; the predominance of the imagination and of the childlike interpretation of things in nature reminds us strikingly of the fancies of children. We find also that the literary remains of this epoch in the world's history, the fairy tales, are the peculiar delight of children from four to six. In like manner the heroic age and its literary products seem to fascinate the children of nine to eleven years. In connection with this theory it is observed that the greatest poets of the world in different countries are those who have given poetic form and expression to the typical ideas and characters of certain epochs of history. So Homer, Virgil, Dante, Milton, Scott. The best literature is, much of it, the precipitate of the thought and life of historical epochs in race development. Experiment has shown that much of this literature is peculiarly adapted to exert strong culture influence upon children. Emerson, in his "Essay on History," says: "What is the foundation of that interest all men feel in Greek history, letters, art, and poetry, in all its periods, from the Heroic or Homeric age down to the domestic life of the Athenians and Spartans, four or five centuries later? What but this, that every man passes personally through a Grecian period?" And again: "The student interprets the age of chivalry by his own age of chivalry, and the days of maritime adventure and circumnavigation by quite parallel miniature experiences of his own. To the sacred history of the world, he has the same key. When the voice of a prophet out of the deeps of antiquity merely echoes to him a sentiment of his infancy, a prayer of his youth, he then pierces to the truth through all the confusion of tradition and the caricature of institutions." The literary heritage of the chief culture epochs is destined therefore to enter as a powerful agent in the education of children in our schools, and the place of a piece of literature in history suggests at least its place in child culture.

The study of these literary masterpieces, the choicest of the world, while it offers a broad perspective of history, also enters deep into the psychology of children and their periods of growth and change. What a study for the teacher!

Suppose now that a wise selection of the best products for school use had been made. The books for each grade would respond not only to the ability but to the characteristic temper and mental status of children at that age. The books would arouse the full compass of the children's mental power, their emotional as well as intellectual capacities, their sympathy, interest, and feeling. The teacher who is about to undertake the training of these children may not know much about children of that age. How can she best put herself into an attitude by which she can meet and understand the children on their own ground? Not simply their intellectual ability and standing, but, better still, their impulses and sympathies, their motives and hearts? Most people, as they reach maturity and advance in years, have a tendency to grow away from their childhood. Their purposes have changed from those of childhood to those of mature life. They are no longer interested in the things that interest children. Such things seem trivial and even incomprehensible to them.

Now the person who is preparing to be a teacher should grow back into his childhood. Without losing the dignity or purpose of mature life, he should allow the memories and sympathies of childhood to revive. The insight which comes from companionship and sympathy with children he needs in order to guide them with tact and wisdom.

The literature which belongs to any age of childhood is perhaps the best key to the spirit and disposition of that period. The fact that it is of permanent worth makes it a fit instrument with which the teacher may reawaken the dormant experiences and memories of that period in his own life. The teacher who finds it impossible to reawaken his interest in the literature that goes home to the hearts of children has *prima facie* evidence that he is not qualified to stimulate and guide their mental movements. The human element in letters is the source of its deep and lasting power; the human element in children is the centre of their educative life, and he who disregards this and thinks only of intellectual exercises is a poor machine. The literature which children appreciate and love is the key to their soul life. It has power to stimulate teacher and pupil alike, and is therefore a common ground where they may both stand and look into each other's faces with sympathy.

This is not so much the statement of a theory as a direct inference from many observations. It has been observed repeatedly, in different schools under many teachers, that the "Lady of the Lake," "Vision of Sir Launfal," "Sleepy Hollow," or "Merchant of Venice" have had an astonishing power to bring teacher and children into near and cherished companionship. It is not possible to express the profound lessons of life that children get from the poets. In the prelude to Whittier's "Among the Hills," what a picture is drawn of the coarse, hard lot of parents and children in an ungarnished home, "so pinched and bare and comfortless," while the poem itself, a view of that home among the hills which thrift and taste and love have made,—

> "Invites the eye to see and heart to feel
> The beauty and the joy within their reach;
> Home and home loves and the beatitudes
> Of nature free to all."

To study such poetry in its effect upon children is a monopoly of the rich educational opportunity which falls naturally into the hands of teachers. Psychology, as derived from text-books, is apt to be cold and formal; that which springs from the contact of young minds with the fountains of song lives and breathes. If a teacher desires to fit herself for primary instruction, she can do nothing so well calculated to bring herself *en rapport* with little children as to read the nursery rhymes, the fairy tales, fables, and early myths. They bring her along a charming road into the realm of childlike fancies and sympathies, which were almost faded from her memory. The same door is opened through well-selected literature to the hearts of children in intermediate and grammar grades.

The sense of humor is cultivated in literature better than elsewhere. In fact, no other study contains much material of humorous quality. A quick sense of it is deemed by many of the best judges an indispensable quality in teachers. Not that a teacher needs to be a diverting story-teller or entertainer, if only he has an indulgent patience and kindly sympathy for those who enjoy telling stories. There is a certain hearty, wholesome social spirit in the enjoyment of humor which diffuses itself like sunlight through a school. It contains an element of kindliness, humanity, and good fellowship which lubricates all the machinery and takes away unnecessary stiffness and gravity in conduct. Best of all it is a sort of mental balance-wheel for the teacher, which enables him to see the ludicrous phases of his own behavior, should he be inclined to run to foolish extremes in various directions. Much of our best literature abounds in humorous elements. Lowell, Holmes, Shakespeare, and Irving are spontaneously rich in this quality of ore, and it is just as well perhaps to cultivate our appreciation in these richer veins as in shallow and unproductive ones elsewhere.

Schlegel says of Shakespeare, his "comic talent is equally wonderful with that he has shown in the pathetic and tragic; it stands at an equal elevation and possesses equal extent and profundity.... Not only has he delineated many kinds of folly, but even of sheer stupidity he has contrived to give a most diverting and entertaining picture."

The inability to appreciate the ludicrous and farcical, and especially of witty conceits, is felt to be a mark of dulness and heaviness, and in dealing with children and young people a versatile perception of the humorous is very helpful. Many of the pupils possess this quality of humor in a marked degree, and the teacher should at least have sufficient insight to appreciate this peculiar bent of mind and turn of wit.

A brief retrospect will make plain the profitableness of classics to the teacher. They show a deep perspective into the spirit and inner workings of history. The social life and insight developed by the study of literature give tact and judgment to understand and respect the many-sided individualities found in every school. The teacher's own moral and æsthetic and religious ideals are constantly lifted and strengthened by the study of classics. Such reading is a recreation and relief even in hours of weariness and solitude. It is an expansive spiritual power rather than a burden. Literary artists are also a standing illustration of the graphic, spirited manner of handling subjects. Finally, this rich and varied realm of classic thought and expression is the doorway by which we enter again into the moods and impulses and fancies of childhood. We thus revive our own youth and fit ourselves for a quick and appreciative perception of children's needs. It is the best kind of child study.

A few of the books which are suggestive, and illustrate the value of literature for teachers, and in some cases even lay out lines of profitable and stimulative reading, are as follows:—

   Newell Dwight Hillis. Great Books and Life Teachers. (Fleming H. Revell Co.)

   George Willis Cooke. Poets and Problems. (Houghton, Mifflin, & Co.)

The Schoolmaster in Literature. (The American Book Co.)

Representative Essays. (G. P. Putnam's Sons.)

Hamilton Wright Mabie. Books and Culture. (Dodd, Mead, & Co.)

James Baldwin. The Book Lover. (A. C. McClurg & Co.)

The Schoolmaster in Comedy and Satire. (The American Book Co.)

Emerson's Essays.

Schlegel's Dramatic Art and Literature. (Bohn's Libraries.)

Ruskin's Sesame and Lilies, and Seven Lamps of Architecture.

Thomas Wentworth Higginson, Book and Heart. (Harper & Brothers.)

Carlyle's Heroes and Hero-Worship.

Counsel upon the Reading of Books. Van Dyke. (Houghton, Mifflin, & Co.)

Literary and General Essays. Charles Kingsley. (Macmillan & Co.)

CHAPTER VII

LIST OF BOOKS

The following list of books, arranged according to grades, is designed to supply the children of the five grades, from the fourth to the eighth inclusive, with excellent reading matter in the form of complete masterpieces of American and English literature. It includes, besides the books for regular reading lessons, a large list of collateral and closely related works for the children and also for teachers.

The books of these lists contain a rich and varied fund of finest culture material, first of all for the teacher, and, through her spirit and enthusiasm, for the children.

Besides the general discussions of these books in the preceding chapters, a few additional explanations are necessary to make plain the grounds upon which this particular selection and arrangement of books is based. The whole purpose of the preceding chapters is to throw light upon this list, and to qualify the teacher for an intelligent and efficient use of these books as school readers.

1. The books apportioned to each grade or year are divided into three series. The first series is carefully selected to serve as regular reading-books for that grade. Almost without exception they are complete works, or collections of complete poems, stories, etc. Many of them are very familiar and have been much used in the schools. The number of books for each grade is large, so as to have room for choice and adaptation to each class.

The second series consists of closely related collateral readings derived from a much wider range of books in literature, history, and science. Many of these books of the second list are not so strictly masterpieces of literature, but of a secondary rank as prose renderings of the great poems, myths, and stories of other languages, also American and European history stories. These materials are well adapted for the reference studies and home readings of children. They all deal with interesting and worthy subjects of thought in a superior style. Many of these books, however, are great and permanent works of literature. They are materials, also, which the teacher should be familiar with. They should be constantly referred to and discussed in connection with the first series. It is quite probable that some teachers will prefer books of the second series for regular reading in the place of some suggested in the first series.

The third series consists of books for teachers, including great works of literature, history, and science, which will enrich the teacher's knowledge and contribute to a broader enthusiasm and culture. The writings of some of the great essayists, as Ruskin, Carlyle, Emerson, Kingsley, Motley, Lowell, Huxley, Macaulay, and others, are peculiarly fit to broaden the teacher's horizon and ennoble his purpose. Some of the best poems and novels suitable for advanced study are mentioned. There are also books which deal in a comprehensive and critical, but sympathetic, way with important literary topics, as the myths and great epics, the age of chivalry, and the lives of the most eminent writers. Some of the best works of biography and history are also suggested for teachers, and a number of the best professional and pedagogical books for teachers, dealing with literature, reading, and child study.

2. This list of books is of course tentative. There are other literary works as good, perhaps, but not a few difficulties stand in the way of the best selection. A few of the best materials are scattered in books not available for school purposes. Some of the finest of our longer classics have not been tested much in school use. There is, however, an abundance of choice English works, complete, well printed and bound, in cheap, schoolbook form. The chief difficulty, after all, is in selecting and arranging the best of an abundant and varied collection of excellent literature. This inspiring problem lies but partly solved at the threshold of every teacher's work. It requires extensive knowledge of literature and experience in its use in classes. A masterpiece may be read in several grades, and teachers will differ in judging its true place. Schools and classes differ also in their capacity and previous preparation for classic readings, so that no course of reading will fit all schools, or, perhaps, any two schools. Many principals will prefer to use the books one or two grades lower, or higher, than here indicated. Every teacher should use such a list according to his best individual judgment as based upon the needs of his school. This list was

discussed and partly made out in conference with a number of experienced superintendents, and much variety of opinion was expressed as to the best grade for the use of a number of the selections.

3. The books chosen for each grade are designed to be a suitable combination of prose and poetry, of short and long selections from history, science, and letters. Variety in subject-matter and style is required in each grade, although certain strong individual characteristics are expected to appear in the literature of each year's work. Many of the shorter poems fit in well with longer masterpieces in prose and verse. Some of the epics, myths, and historical episodes are told in both prose and verse. The children may well meet and study them in both forms. If from four to six larger masterpieces could be read each year, and these could bring out the style and quality of so many authors, if a number of suitable shorter pieces could be read and related to the former, the many-sided influence of literature would prove each year effective. Literature is the broadest of all subjects, both as a basis of culture and for the unification of the varied studies. It touches every phase of experience and knowledge along its higher levels, and overlooks the whole field of life from the standpoint of the seer and poet. The classic readings should aim at the completeness, variety, and elevation of thought which literature alone can give. Every year's literature should open the gates to meadow and woodland, to park and fruitful fields, into rich and shaded valleys, and up to free and sunny hilltops and mountains.

4. The list of books for each year includes two or three books of miscellaneous collections of classics in prose and verse. Many of the selections are short and some fragmentary. Such are the three volumes of "Open Sesame," the "Golden Treasury of Songs and Lyrics," "Children's Treasury of English Song," and "Book of Golden Deeds." In each of the books named is found a variety of material suited perhaps to two or three grades. In most of the books just named it is not intended in our plan that all the selections should be read through in succession. It will be better for the teacher to select from those collections such choice poems, stories, etc., as will enrich and supplement the longer classics, and give that added variety so needful. Many of the finest poems in our language are short, and should not be omitted from our school course. They should be read and some of them memorized by the children. It would be well if the teacher had in each

grade one or two sets of such books of choice miscellaneous materials from which to select occasional reading. The regular readers used by the children would consist of the longer masterpieces, which would be supplemented by the shorter selections. In this way greater unity and variety might be achieved within the limits of each grade.

5. Information books and supplementary readers in history, geography, and natural science have been excluded, in the main, from our lists. The test of literary excellence has been applied to most of the books chosen. De Quincey's distinction between the literature of knowledge and that of power is our line of demarkation. It seems to us probable that the future will call for a still more stringent adherence to this principle of selection. Information readers are good and necessary in their place in geography, history, and natural science; but they are not good enough to take the place of classics in reading lessons. The only exceptions to the rule of classics are the prose renderings of the old classics, as the "Story of the Odyssey," and the biographical stories from history. Both these have so much of interest and stimulus for the young that they seem to harmonize with our plan. But criticism may yet expose their inadequacy.

It is our plan, in brief, to limit the reading work mainly to the choice masterpieces of the best authors, and to render these studies as fruitful as possible in spiritual power. If supplementary readings are used at all, let them be those which will strengthen the influence of the classics.

It has been our plan to collect in the Special Method Books devoted to geography, history, and natural science, a full list of the supplementary readers and information books in those subjects.

6. In our list, however, is included quite a number of classic renderings of science and nature topics. Such are "Wake Robin," "Birds and Bees," "A Hunting of the Deer," etc., "Sharp Eyes" etc., "Succession of Forest Trees," "Up and Down the Brooks," "Water Babies," "The Foot-path Way," "Madam How and Lady Why," "Wilderness Ways," "In Bird Land," and many others.

These books, however, belong to the literature of power. They look at nature through the eyes of poet and artist and enthusiast. They are not cold, matter-of-fact delineations. They unfold the æsthetic and human side of nature, the divinity of flower and tree. These books are the communings of the soul with nature, and are closely related in spirit to the poems of nature in Bryant, Wordsworth, Tennyson, and other poets. There has been a chasm between them and our text-books in science which needs bridging over. Now that science is beginning to be taught objectively, experimentally, and inductively, there will be much less of a hiatus at this stage, because there is so much that is powerfully stimulating in nature study.

7. Some books are named twice in the lists, first as books of reference, or in the teacher's lists, and in a later grade for the use of children in regular reading. We have been especially careful in selecting appropriate books in the first list for each grade adapted to the age of the children. These books for regular reading must be used by every child, so that they should be fitted to the average ability. The reference books for collateral reading in the second series of each grade may be more difficult in some cases, as they will be used, in part, only by the stronger pupils.

There are certain groups of kindred books, like the Greek myths, that are distributed through three or more grades. It is not expected that any child will use all of these books, as several of them may deal with the same story, like the "Iliad" or "Odyssey." It seemed best to include all the important renderings of these stories, and leave the teacher to choose among them for his class.

8. To give more specific aid to teachers, most of the books are briefly described, and some notion of their special worth and fitness indicated. It is hoped that these short descriptions will be of considerable help to young teachers in making selections for their classes.

9. Many of the best and most commonly used books are published by several companies. In such cases the names of the different publishers are indicated in connection with each book.

10. By an examination of these lists the teacher of any grade will discover that, in order to teach well, she must be acquainted with the books used in one or two grades, both above and below her own. All the chief groups of books in literature run through three or four grades, and the teacher in any grade needs to get a comprehensive view of the important groups of books used in her classes. In addition to this, the books

recommended for teachers give a still more definite and comprehensive grasp of large classes of literary material. The books recommended for teachers could be indefinitely extended, but it is hoped that enough are mentioned to give definiteness to their wider studies, and to serve as an introduction to some of the larger fields of literature, science, and history.

11. There are certain peculiar difficulties connected with the reading of longer classics which are much less frequently met with in the usual school readers. These difficulties are of such a real and serious kind that many teachers are apt to be discouraged before success is attained. Complete classics like Webster's speeches, "Julius Cæsar," "Snow-Bound," "Marmion," and "Evangeline" have been regarded as too long and difficult for school purposes. We have found, however, that the greater length, if rightly utilized, only intensifies the effect of a masterpiece. The chief objection is the greater language difficulty (hard and unusual words, proper names, etc.) of the longer classics. This is a real obstacle and must be fairly met. It is impossible to grade down the language and thought of a great writer. It is necessary to bring the class up to his level rather than bring him down to theirs. This requires time and skill and perseverance on the teacher's part, and labor and thought in the children. It may require a week or a month to get a class well under way in "Lady of the Lake," "King of the Golden River," or the "Sketch-Book." But when well done it is a conquest of no mean importance. The language, style, and characteristics of the author are strange and difficult. The scales must drop from children's eyes before they will appreciate Ruskin or Tennyson or Emerson. The wings of fancy, the æsthetic sense, do not unfold in a single day. But if these initial difficulties can be overcome, we shall emerge soon into the sunlight of interest and success. It takes a degree of faith in good things and patience under difficulties to attain success in classic readings. Even when the teacher thinks he is doing fairly well, the parents sometimes say the work is too hard and the verbal difficulties too great. Generally, however, parents are satisfied when children work hard and are interested.

Again, children whose reading in the lower grades has been of the information order lack the imaginative power that is essential to the grasp and enjoyment of any masterpiece. The sleeping or dulled fancy must be awakened. The power to image things, so natural to the poet, must be aroused and exercised. The lack of training in vivid and poetic thought in early years is sure to make itself felt in deficient and languid thought and feeling in the higher grades. But we cannot afford to give up the struggle. We may be forced to begin lower down in the series of books, but anything less than a classic is not fit for the children.

12. The leading publishing houses are now competing vigorously in bringing out the best complete classics in cheap, durable, well-printed form for school use. In our list the names of the publishers are given. Most of the companies can be addressed in Boston, Chicago, New York, or San Francisco. Most of the books bound in boards or cloth range in price from twenty-five to fifty cents. The pamphlet editions are from ten to fifteen cents. The larger books of miscellaneous collections and some of the science classics range from seventy-five cents to a dollar and a quarter. A few of the books are priced as high as two dollars.

13. Before final publication, the following lists of books have been submitted to the criticism of a number of able superintendents and to the leading publishing houses. In consequence considerable changes and additions have been made. The chief criticism offered was that the books, in a number of cases, are too difficult for the grades indicated. To meet this objection a few changes were made, while in several cases books are described as suitable for two or three grades.

For the sake of quick and easy reference in finding any book, an alphabetical list of the titles of all the books is given at the close, and the page indicated where each book may be found in the descriptive list.

FOURTH GRADE

1. BOOKS FOR REGULAR READING LESSONS

Hawthorne's Wonder Book. Houghton, Mifflin, & Co.; Educational Publishing Co.

> Has been very extensively used in fourth and fifth grades, and even in sixth. A book of standard excellence.

Kingsley's Greek Heroes. Ginn & Co.; The Macmillan Co.

> Much used. Excellent. Covers much the same ground as the Wonder Book and is preferred by some to it.

Stories from the Arabian Nights. Houghton, Mifflin, & Co.

> Excellent. It contains some of the most familiar stories, as Aladdin, in simple form.

Whittier's Child Life in Poetry and Prose. Houghton, Mifflin, & Co.

> An excellent selection of poems and stories of child life by Whittier. It has many simple poems and stories, as Barefoot Boy, John Gilpin, etc. Also for fifth grade.

Fanciful Tales (Stockton). Scribner's Sons.

> Very pleasing and well-told stories for children. It has not been extensively used for reading as yet.

Book of Tales. American Book Co.

> A good collection of old fairy tales, stories, and poems. It has been extensively used.

Old Testament Stories in Scripture Language. Houghton, Mifflin, & Co. Abraham, Joseph, Moses, and others.

> The patriarchal stories in familiar Bible language. It may be a little difficult for the first part of the year.

Round the Year in Myth and Song (Holbrook). American Book Co.

> A fine collection of nature poems for occasional use throughout the year.

Bird-World (Stickney-Hoffman). Ginn & Co.

> An interesting collection of bird stories and descriptions. Simple. A good book to encourage observation of birds.

Nature in Verse (Lovejoy). Silver, Burdett, & Co.

> An excellent collection of nature poems arranged by the seasons.

Book of Legends (Scudder). Houghton, Mifflin, & Co.

Andersen's Fairy Tales. First and Second Series. Ginn & Co.

Grimm's Household Tales. Houghton, Mifflin, & Co.

Four Great Americans (Baldwin). Werner School Book Co.

Hans Andersen Tales. The Macmillan Co.

Squirrels and Other Fur-Bearers (Burroughs). Houghton, Mifflin, & Co.

> Very entertaining, but somewhat difficult in language. Use toward the end of the year, and in fifth grade.

Peabody's Old Greek Folk Stories. Houghton, Mifflin, & Co.

> Simple and well written. It supplements the Wonder Book.

King Arthur and his Court (Greene). Ginn & Co.

> A recent book. Simple in style and pleasing to children.

The Howells Story Book. Scribner's Sons.

2. SUPPLEMENTARY AND REFERENCE BOOKS

Stories of Our Country (Johonnot). American Book Co.

    Good American stories for children to read at home or school.

Tales from the "Faerie Queene." The Macmillan Co.

    For reference and library.

Bimbi (De la Ramée). Ginn & Co.

    The Nürnberg Stove and other good stories. Good for home reading and for school work.

The Nürnberg Stove. Maynard, Merrill, & Co.; Houghton, Mifflin, & Co.

Gods and Heroes (Francillon). Ginn & Co.

    Suitable to late fourth and fifth grades for collateral reading. Simple in style.

Waste Not, Want Not (Edgeworth). Ginn & Co.; D. C. Heath, & Co.; Houghton, Mifflin, & Co.

    Practical stories for children, illustrating foresight, economy, etc.

A Ballad Book (Bates). Sibley & Ducker.

    A good collection of the older, simpler ballads. These ballads should be distributed through the year. Good for supplementary reading, also for drill in reading.

The Story of Ulysses (Cook). Public School Publishing Co.

    An excellent rendering, sometimes used as a reader.

Friends and Helpers (Eddy). Ginn & Co.

    Stories of animals and birds. Instructive.

Hans Andersen Stories. Houghton, Mifflin, & Co.

Tommy-Anne and the Three Hearts (Wright). The Macmillan Co.

First Book of Birds (Miller). Houghton, Mifflin, & Co.

    Very simple and interesting descriptions and accounts of common birds. Will help to interest the children in nature.

The Little Lame Prince. Maynard, Merrill, & Co.; D. C. Heath & Co.

    A story for home reading.

The Dog of Flanders. Maynard, Merrill, & Co.; Houghton, Mifflin, & Co.; Educational Publishing Co.

    An excellent story for children to read at home or in school. Pathetic.

Old Stories of the East (Baldwin). American Book Co.

    A pleasing treatment of the old Bible stories, not in Bible language. Well written.

Fairy Tales in Prose and Verse (Rolfe). American Book Co.

>A choice collection of stories and poems.

Heroes of Asgard. The Macmillan Co.

>A good simple treatment of the Norse myths. Suitable for supplementary and sight reading.

Tales of Troy (De Garmo). Public School Publishing Co.

>A simple narrative of the Trojan war. Supplementary.

Our Feathered Friends (Grinnell). D. C. Heath & Co.

>Instructive book on birds.

Alice's Adventures in Wonderland (Carroll). The Macmillan Co.; Educational Publishing Co.

>Very suitable for home and family reading. Younger children enjoy it much. Entertaining.

Jackanapes, The Brownies (Mrs. Ewing). Houghton, Mifflin, & Co.

Through the Looking Glass (Carroll). The Macmillan Co.; Educational Publishing Co.

The Merry Adventures of Robin Hood (Pyle). Scribner's Sons.

>An expensive book (about three dollars). Excellent stories to read to children. Full of humor and adventure. Finely illustrated. A good book for school and home library.

Open Sesame, Vol. I and Vol. II. Ginn & Co.

>A fine collection of the best poems of nature, heroism, Christmas time, etc. Ballads and stories. They are adapted to children in several grades, and should be used for reading, memory work, and for recitation.

Stories of the Old World (Church). Ginn & Co.

>Good reading matter for fourth and fifth grades. Interesting for supplementary reading.

Stories of American Life and Adventure (Eggleston). American Book Co.

Black Beauty. Educational Publishing Co.; University Pub. Co.

Children's Treasury of English Song. The Macmillan Co.

>A collection of poems for occasional use.

Little Lord Fauntleroy. Scribner's Sons.

>A famous story for home reading. A book for libraries.

Heroes of the Middle West (Catherwood). Ginn & Co.

>Stories for later fourth and fifth grades. A good book for supplementary reading. Also for sixth grade.

Old Norse Stories (Bradish). American Book Co.

>Stories for reference reading and sight reading.

Stories from Plato (Burt). Ginn & Co.

 Simple myths and stories for home reading.

The Eugene Field Book. Scribner's Sons.

 Pleasing and entertaining for younger children. Prose and verse, humorous and pathetic.

Stories from Old Germany (Pratt). Educational Publishing Co.

A simple, interesting rendering of the story of Siegfried.

Secrets of the Woods. Ginn & Co.

Norse Stories (Mabie). Dodd, Mead, & Co.

An excellent rendering of the Norse stories. Simple.

Fifty Famous Stories Retold (Baldwin). American Book Co.

Simple and well told.

Pioneers of the Revolution. Public School Publishing Co.

A simple narrative of pioneer life and conflict in the South-west during the Revolution.

3. TEACHERS' BOOKS

Story of the Iliad (Church). The Macmillan Co.

A reference book for outside reading.

Emerson's Essays. Second Series. Houghton, Mifflin, & Co.

Essays on the poet, manners, character, etc. Inspiring reading for the teacher.

Myths of the Northern Lands (Guerber). American Book Co.

Readings in Folklore (Skinner). American Book Co.

Good general introduction to the folklore of modern European countries.

History and Literature (Rice). A. Flanagan.

A discussion of books and materials for teachers.

Being a Boy (Warner). Houghton, Mifflin, & Co.

David Copperfield (Charles Dickens).

Talks to Teachers (James).

Sesame and Lilies (Ruskin). Houghton, Mifflin, & Co.; The Macmillan Co.

Tales of a Traveler (Irving). American Book Co.; Maynard, Merrill, & Co.

Poetry for Children (Eliot). Houghton, Mifflin, & Co.

A good collection for miscellaneous uses in the school.

California and Oregon Trail (Parkman). Hurst & Co.; Little, Brown, & Co.

Interesting descriptions of Indian and Western life.

Story of the Odyssey (Church). The Macmillan Co.

Good for reference and general reading.

Literature in Schools (Scudder). Houghton, Mifflin, & Co.

>A series of three excellent papers on the use and value of literature in schools. Especially valuable for teachers.

Children's Stories of American Literature (Wright). Scribner's.

>Short biographies of American writers in two small volumes.

The Age of Fable (Bulfinch). Lee & Shepard.

>One of the best general treatises on mythology.

National Epics (Rabb). A. C. McClurg.

>A good introduction and extracts from the great epic poems of all nations.

In Bird Land (Keyser). A. C. McClurg.

>Delightful reading and suggestive to teachers.

The Ways of Wood Folk (Long). Ginn & Co.

>Very pleasing stories of animal life for children and teachers.

Nature Pictures by American Poets (Marble). The Macmillan Co.

La Salle and the Discovery of the Great West (Parkman). Little, Brown, & Co.

>Very interesting account of the exploration of the Great Lakes and the Mississippi River.

The Discovery of America, two volumes (Fiske). Houghton, Mifflin, & Co.

>Valuable account of Columbus and other explorers.

The Beginnings of New England (Fiske). Houghton, Mifflin, & Co.

>Excellent.

The Story-Teller's Art (Dye). Ginn & Co.

>A book designed for high school teachers, but good also for teachers in the grades.

The Winning of the West (Roosevelt). Putnam.

Leonard and Gertrude (Pestalozzi). D. C. Heath & Co.

Jean Mitchell's School. Public School Publishing Co.

The Pilot (Cooper). American Book Co.; University Pub. Co.

FIFTH GRADE

1. BOOKS FOR REGULAR READING LESSONS

Hiawatha. Houghton, Mifflin, & Co.; The Macmillan Co.; Educational Publishing Co.; University Pub. Co.

Well suited for reading. Used in several grades.

Lays of Ancient Rome (Macaulay). Maynard, Merrill, & Co.; Houghton, Mifflin, & Co.; The Macmillan Co.; Educational Publishing Co.; American Book Co.

The four ballad poems. Good school reading for children. Names somewhat hard at first. Very stimulating and heroic. Used also in sixth grade.

King of the Golden River (Ruskin). Ginn & Co.; The Macmillan Co.; Houghton, Mifflin, & Co.; D. C. Heath & Co.; Maynard, Merrill, & Co.

Much used. Excellent story and reading.

Tanglewood Tales (Hawthorne). Houghton, Mifflin, & Co.

Companion book to the Wonder Book. Excellent matter for reading.

Water Babies (Kingsley). Ginn & Co.; The Macmillan Co.; Educational Publishing Co.; Maynard, Merrill, & Co.

Interesting story. Good also for home reading. Better, perhaps, for sixth grade.

Ulysses among the Phæacians (Bryant). Houghton, Mifflin, & Co.

Simple and easy. Poetic in its rendering. Better for sixth grade in some classes.

Tales from English History (prose and verse). American Book Company.

Stories and ballads of the leading periods of English history from the best authors. Illustrated.

Gulliver's Travels. Houghton, Mifflin, & Co.; Ginn & Co.; The Macmillan Co.; Educational Publishing Co.

Somewhat difficult in spots. Very interesting to boys and girls. For some classes use in sixth grade.

Adventures of Ulysses (Lamb). Ginn & Co.; D. C. Heath & Co.

Well told, giving complete outline of the whole story.

Heroic Ballads. Ginn & Co.

Scotch and English and many later and American ballads.

The Pied Piper and Other Poems (Browning). Houghton, Mifflin, & Co.

Also other poems and ballads of Browning.

Tales from Scottish History (Rolfe). American Book Co.

Some Merry Adventures of Robin Hood (Pyle). Scribner's Sons. Shorter School Edition.

Humorous and entertaining.

Little Daffydowndilly and Biographical Stories (Hawthorne). Houghton, Mifflin, & Co. The latter for sixth grade.

Stories of American Life and Adventure (Eggleston). American Book Co.

The Ways of Wood Folk (Long). Ginn & Co.

> An excellent nature book for children, entertaining, instructive, and well written.

Gulliver's Voyage to Lilliput (Swift). Maynard, Merrill, & Co.

Squirrels and Other Fur-Bearers (Burroughs). Houghton, Mifflin, & Co.

The Children's Hour (Longfellow). Houghton, Mifflin, & Co.

2. SUPPLEMENTARY AND REFERENCE BOOKS

Arabian Nights (Hale). Ginn & Co.

> Many of the best stories of the collection, including a number of the less familiar ones. Also for regular reading.

Ten Boys on the Road from Long Ago. Ginn & Co.

> A book interesting and much used. Good for reading in fourth, fifth, and sixth grades. Also for sight reading.

Robinson Crusoe. Ginn & Co.; D. C. Heath & Co.; American Book Co.; University Publishing Co.

> Much reduced and simplified from the original. A complete and more difficult edition is published by Houghton, Mifflin, & Co.

The Odyssey of Homer (Palmer). Houghton, Mifflin, & Co.

> A complete prose translation of the entire Odyssey. Probably the best. Good for fifth and sixth grades.

Bryant's Odyssey. Houghton, Mifflin, & Co.

> A simple, poetic rendering of the whole Odyssey. A good teacher's book. Use parts in class.

Bryant's Iliad. Houghton, Mifflin, & Co.

> Complete poetic translation. One of the best.

Heroes of the Middle West (Catherwood). Ginn & Co.

> Good stories of the early French explorers of the Great Lakes and the Mississippi Valley. Somewhat difficult.

Pope's Iliad. The Macmillan Co.; Ginn & Co.; American Book Co.; Silver, Burdett, & Co.; D. C. Heath & Co.

> A famous rendering of the old Greek story. Still better for sixth grade.

A Story of the Golden Age (Baldwin). Scribner's Sons.

Secrets of the Woods (Long). Ginn & Co.

Old Greek Story (Baldwin). American Book Co.

Arabian Nights (Clarke). American Book Co.

Colonial Children (Hart). The Macmillan Co.

> Simple and well-chosen source material. Excellent.

Krag and Johnny Bear (Seton). Scribner's Sons.

Poems of American Patriotism (Matthews). Scribner's Sons.

Ballads and Lyrics. Houghton, Mifflin, & Co.

Stories from Herodotus. Maynard, Merrill & Co.; The Macmillan Co.

> Simple and interesting stories. Good also for sixth grade.

Jason's Quest. Sibley & Ducker.

> The story of Jason told in full. Interesting and well written.

Book of Golden Deeds. The Macmillan Co.

> A fine collection of historical and famous stories. For sixth grade also.

Historical Tales, American (Morris). J. B. Lippincott.

> One of the best collections of American stories.

Greek Gods, Heroes, and Men. Scott, Foresman, & Co.

> A collection of Greek stories, both mythical and historical.

The Story of the English (Guerber). American Book Co.

> A complete series of English history stories arranged chronologically, good for fifth and sixth grades.

Tales of Chivalry (Rolfe). American Book Co.

> Good stories from Scott, mostly from Ivanhoe. Also the early life of Scott. Good for fifth and sixth grades.

Boy's King Arthur (Lanier). Scribner's Sons.

> A very interesting story for boys and girls. A good library book ($2.00).

The Story of Siegfried (Baldwin). Scribner's Sons.

> A full and attractive story of Siegfried's adventures. A good library book ($2.00).

Pioneer History Stories (McMurry). Three volumes. The Macmillan Co. Also for sixth year.

> Early pioneer stories of the Eastern states, of the Mississippi Valley, and of the Rocky Mountains.

Open Sesame. Part II. Ginn & Co.

> A good collection of poems arranged in important classes.

The Story of the Greeks (Guerber). American Book Co.

> Leading stories of Greek myth and history. For fifth and sixth grades.

The Story of Troy. American Book Co.

    A short narrative of the Trojan War.

Story of the Odyssey (Church). The Macmillan Co.

    Library book for general reading. Simple.

The Story of Roland (Baldwin). Scribner's Sons.

    Large book for library. Good.

The Hoosier School Boy (Eggleston). Scribner's Sons.

American Explorers (Higginson). Lee & Shepard.

    Excellent descriptions of early explorations. Good source material for pupils and teachers. Also for sixth grade.

The Children's Life of Abraham Lincoln (Putnam). A. C. McClurg. Also for sixth and seventh grades.

Four American Naval Heroes (Beebe). Werner School Book Company. Sixth grade also.

    A simple narrative of great naval conflicts.

Lobo, Rag, and Vixen (Seton). Scribner's Sons.

3. TEACHERS' BOOKS

Beginnings of New England and Discovery of America, two volumes (Fiske). Houghton, Mifflin, & Co.

    Good library books for teacher.

Sesame and Lilies (Ruskin). The Macmillan Co.

    A very stimulating and suggestive book for teachers.

The Golden Age (Kenneth and Grahame). John Lane.

Moral Instruction of Children (Adler). D. Appleton & Co.

Childhood in Literature and Art (Scudder). Houghton, Mifflin, & Co.

    An instructive book for teachers.

Readings in Folk Lore (Skinner). American Book Co.

    Valuable source book.

Wilderness Ways (Long). Ginn & Co.

    Entertaining to both teachers and pupils.

The Story of Our Continent (Shaler). Ginn & Co.

    An interesting geological history of North America.

Historical Tales, English (Morris). J. B. Lippincott.

> Excellent materials for reference work.

Westward Ho! (Kingsley). The Macmillan Co.; University Publishing Co.

> A good story of the time of Elizabeth, Drake, and Raleigh.

Samuel de Champlain (Sedgwick). Houghton, Mifflin, & Co.

> A short and interesting biography. Other books of the same Riverside Biographical Series are, William Penn, Lewis and Clark, George Rogers Clark, and Paul Jones.

History and Literature (Rice). Flanagan.

> A brief pedagogical treatment of the whole subject of literature and history for the elementary school.

Ivanhoe (Scott). Ginn & Co.; D. C. Heath & Co.; Houghton, Mifflin, & Co.; American Book Co.; The Macmillan Co.

The Deerslayer (Cooper). The Macmillan Co.

House of Seven Gables (Hawthorne). Houghton, Mifflin, & Co.

Drake and his Yeomen (Barnes). The Macmillan Co.

Hard Times (Charles Dickens).

> Mechanical methods in education described.

Wake Robin (Burroughs). Houghton, Mifflin, & Co.

> A book of pleasing nature observation and study.

Pioneers of France in the New World, and La Salle and the Discovery of the Great West (Parkman). Little, Brown, & Co.

> Excellent and interesting historical material for the teacher.

The Men Who Made the Nation (Sparks). The Macmillan Co.

> Interesting biographical material.

The Age of Chivalry (Bulfinch). Lee & Shepard.

> An important treatise on this subject. Library book.

The Foot-path Way (Torrey). Houghton, Mifflin, & Co.

> Attractive and inspiring nature study.

Birddom (Keyser). Lothrop & Co.

> Excellent style and treatment of bird life.

News from the Birds (Keyser). D. Appleton & Co.

> Very pleasing studies and stimulating to teachers.

Greek Life and Story (Church). G. P. Putnam's Sons.

> A good series of pictures from the chief episodes of Greek history.

Counsel upon the Reading of Books (Van Dyke). Houghton, Mifflin, & Co. Excellent.

The Odyssey (Butcher and Lang). The Macmillan Co.

SIXTH GRADE

1. BOOKS FOR REGULAR READING LESSONS

The Sketch-Book (Irving). Ginn & Co.; American Book Co.; Maynard, Merrill, & Co.; Macmillan Co.; Houghton, Mifflin, & Co.; Educational Pub. Co.; University Pub. Co.

> Rip Van Winkle and other American essays. One of the best books for sixth grade. Used also in fifth and seventh grades.

The Courtship of Miles Standish (Longfellow). Houghton, Mifflin, & Co.

> Excellent in many ways for sixth-grade children. A dramatized edition is also published. Used sometimes in seventh grade.

The Christmas Carol (Dickens). Houghton, Mifflin, & Co.; Maynard, Merrill, & Co.; Educational Publishing Co.

> Excellent as literature and for variety of style in class work. Used also in seventh grade.

Hunting of the Deer (Warner). Houghton, Mifflin, & Co.

> Including also How I Killed a Bear, and other admirable stories, in which the humor and sentiment are fine. Used also in seventh grade.

Snow-Bound and Songs of Labor (Whittier). Houghton, Mifflin, & Co.

> One of the best American poems for children. Used also in seventh and eighth grades.

Coming of Arthur and Passing of Arthur. Houghton, Mifflin, & Co.; Maynard, Merrill, & Co.; The Macmillan Co.

> In the fine, poetic style of Tennyson, but simple. Suited also for seventh grade.

The Gentle Boy and Other Tales (Hawthorne). Houghton, Mifflin, & Co.

> A pathetic story of the Quaker persecutions in New England.

Tales of the White Hills and Sketches (Hawthorne). Houghton, Mifflin, & Co.

> The Great Stone Face in this series is one of the choicest stories for children in English.

Plutarch's Alexander the Great. Houghton, Mifflin, & Co.

> A good biography for children and serves well as an introduction to Plutarch.

Grandfather's Chair (Hawthorne). Houghton, Mifflin, & Co.

The best stories we have of early and colonial New England history. Good also for seventh grade.

Children's Hour, Paul Revere, and other papers (Longfellow). Houghton, Mifflin, & Co.

This contains also the Birds of Killingworth, and other of Longfellow's best short poems.

Birds and Bees, Sharp Eyes, and other papers (Burroughs). Houghton, Mifflin, & Co. Also for seventh grade.

These are among the best of Burroughs's books for children. Classic in style and choice in matter.

Hawthorne's Biographical Stories. Houghton, Mifflin, & Co.

Seven American Classics (Swinton). American Book Co.

A good collection of American classics suited to this grade.

Three Outdoor Papers (Higginson). Houghton, Mifflin, & Co.

Interesting studies of nature in choice style.

Giles Corey (Longfellow). Houghton, Mifflin, & Co.

A drama of the Salem witchcraft, with directions for its representation on the stage.

The Building of the Ship, The Masque of Pandora, and other poems (Longfellow). Houghton, Mifflin, & Co.

Excellent. The Masque of Pandora could be rendered in dramatic form by children. Also for seventh grade.

Mabel Martin and other poems (Whittier). Houghton, Mifflin, & Co.

A choice collection of poems from Whittier. A good picture of New England life. Used also in seventh and eighth grades.

Baby Bell, The Little Violinist, and other prose and verse (Aldrich). Houghton, Mifflin, & Co.

Very choice poems and stories.

Open Sesame, Vol. II, and Vol. III. Ginn & Co.

Poems and ballads. A collection well arranged for various school use, for reading, recitation, and memorizing.

2. SUPPLEMENTARY AND REFERENCE BOOKS

Ten Great Events in History (Johonnot). D. Appleton & Co.

Good collateral reading in this grade.

Lanier's Froissart. Scribner's Sons.

A fine story for library ($2.00).

Child's History of England (Dickens). Hurst & Co.; Houghton, Mifflin, & Co.; American Book Co.

A book much used. Should be in a school library.

Tales from Shakespeare (Lamb). American Book Co.; Macmillan Co.; Educational Publishing Co.; D. C. Heath & Co.; Houghton, Mifflin, & Co.

Designed as an introduction to the plays of Shakespeare. Language and style superior. Used also in seventh grade.

Pilgrim's Progress (Bunyan). Macmillan Co.; Ginn & Co.; Houghton, Mifflin, & Co.; University Publishing Co.

The famous old story which all children should read. A book for the library and the home.

Story of Cæsar (Clarke). American Book Co.

Heroes and Patriots of the Revolution (Hart). The Macmillan Co.

Swiss Family Robinson. Ginn & Co.; Educational Publishing Co.

A library book for children. University Publishing Co.

Stories from Old English Poetry (Richardson). Houghton, Mifflin, & Co.

An excellent series of stories from Chaucer and others.

Historical Tales, English (Morris). J. B. Lippincott.

A good collection of English history stories.

Selections from Irving. Sibley & Ducker.

A variety of interesting selections from Irving's works.

The Conquest of Mexico (Prescott). Maynard, Merrill, & Co.

The story of Cortes and his adventures told by a master.

William Tell (McMurry). Silver, Burdett, & Co.

The drama of Schiller's Wilhelm Tell, translated into simple English. Adapted for representation.

Source Book of American History (Hart). Macmillan Co.

The parts bearing on the colonial history. Original sources, letters, etc.

Story of a Bad Boy (Aldrich). Houghton, Mifflin, & Co.

A good narrative of boy life, humorous and entertaining.

Lay of the Last Minstrel (Scott). The Macmillan Co.; Maynard, Merrill, & Co.; Ginn & Co.; Houghton, Mifflin, & Co.

One of the best descriptions of the old minstrelsy. Suitable for sixth and seventh grades.

Choice English Lyrics (Baldwin). Silver, Burdett, & Co.

A great variety of choice poems, ballads, lyrics, and sonnets.

Poetry of the Seasons (Lovejoy). Silver, Burdett, & Co.

A choice collection of nature poems.

Wilderness Ways (Long). Ginn & Co.

An interesting study of wild animals, birds, etc.

Famous Allegories (Baldwin). Silver, Burdett, & Co.

A good selection for reference reading and for teachers.

Rab and His Friends (Brown). Educational Publishing Co.; D. C. Heath & Co.; Houghton, Mifflin, & Co.

Interesting stories of dogs for children.

Story of Oliver Twist (Dickens). D. Appleton & Co.

Suitable for introducing children to Dickens.

Undine (Fouque). Ginn & Co.

Nine Worlds (Litchfield). Ginn & Co.

Hans Brinker, or the Silver Skates (Mary Mapes Dodge). Century Co.

Don Quixote (De la Mancha). Scribner's Sons; Ginn & Co.

Tales of a Traveller (Irving). American Book Co.; Maynard, Merrill, & Co.

Various interesting stories of adventure.

Pilgrims and Puritans (Moore). Ginn & Co.

One of the best books on the early history of Plymouth and Boston. Very simple and well told.

Stories from Waverley (Gassiot). The Macmillan Co.

For reference reading. Stories from Scott.

Golden Treasury of Songs and Lyrics (Palgrave). The Macmillan Co.

A collection of the best songs and lyrical poems.

The Rose and the Ring (Thackeray). D. C. Heath & Co.

Knickerbocker Stories. University Publishing Co.

Boys of '76 (Coffin). Harper Brothers.

A realistic account of Revolutionary scenes.

Stories of Bird Life (Pearson). B. F. Johnson Publishing Co.

Simple descriptions by a close observer of birds.

Our Country in Prose and Verse. American Book Co.

Excellent collection for children's use.

Stories of Animal Life (Holden). American Book Co.

Stories from English History (Church). The Macmillan Co.

> In two volumes. The second part is especially suited to sixth grade. Parts also of Part One.

Children's Stories of American Literature (Wright). 1660-1860. Scribner's Sons.

> Short biographies of the chief American writers.

Golden Arrow (Hall). Houghton, Mifflin, & Co.

3. TEACHERS' BOOKS

Peter the Great (Motley). Maynard, Merrill, & Co.

> A very interesting essay for teachers and for older pupils.

Frederick the Great (Macaulay). Maynard, Merrill, & Co.

> For teachers only. Interesting in style and content.

Life Histories of American Insects (Weed). The Macmillan Co.

> An interesting scientific treatment.

Vicar of Wakefield (Goldsmith). Ginn & Co.; American Book Co.; D. C. Heath & Co.; Houghton, Mifflin, & Co.; The Macmillan Co.; The University Publishing Co.

The Talisman (Scott). American Book Co.; Ginn & Co.

Introduction to Literature (Lewis). The Macmillan Co.

> Good selections.

Source Book of English History (Kendall). The Macmillan Co.

> Good selections for sixth, seventh, and eighth grades.

Twice Told Tales (Hawthorne). Houghton, Mifflin, & Co.

Old Virginia and Her Neighbors, two volumes (Fiske). Houghton, Mifflin, & Co.

The Dutch and Quaker Colonies in America, two volumes (Fiske). Houghton, Mifflin, & Co.

> These four volumes are excellent for the treatment of colonial history.

An Introduction to Ruskin. Sibley & Ducker.

> Extracts from Ruskin's principal writings.

Essay on Milton (Macaulay). Maynard, Merrill, & Co.; American Book Co.; The Macmillan Co.

> A good example of Macaulay's style.

History of England (Macaulay). Maynard, Merrill, & Co.

> A brief history of England from the earliest times to 1660.

The Iliad (Bryant). Houghton, Mifflin, & Co.

Books and Libraries (Lowell). Houghton, Mifflin, & Co.

> A valuable and interesting essay on libraries and books. Also other essays.

The Red Cross Story Book (Lang). Longmans & Co.

Montcalm and Wolfe (Parkman). Little, Brown, & Co.

Washington Irving (Warner). Houghton, Mifflin, & Co.

> Of the American Men of Letters Series.

Conspiracy of Pontiac (Parkman). Little, Brown, & Co.

The Fortune of the Republic (Emerson). Houghton, Mifflin, & Co.

Nature Pictures by American Poets (Marble). The Macmillan Co.

> A choice collection of nature poems.

Poetic Interpretation of Nature (Shairp). Houghton, Mifflin, & Co.

> An interesting treatise on the sources of poetry in nature.

Westward Ho! (Kingsley). The Macmillan Co.; The University Publishing Co.

> A story of the time of Elizabeth.

The Schoolmaster in Literature. American Book Co.

Also its companion book, The Schoolmaster in Comedy and Satire. American Book Co.

Scarlet Letter (Hawthorne).

Last of the Mohicans (Cooper). D. C. Heath & Co.; Houghton, Mifflin, & Co.; Macmillan Co.; University Pub. Co.

Henry Esmond (Thackeray). Houghton, Mifflin; Macmillan.

Nicholas Nickleby (Charles Dickens).

SEVENTH GRADE

1. BOOKS FOR REGULAR READING LESSONS

Evangeline (Longfellow). Houghton, Mifflin, & Co.; The Macmillan Co.; The University Publishing Co.

> This has been much used in seventh and eighth grades.

Sella, Thanatopsis, and Other Poems (Bryant). Houghton, Mifflin, & Co.; Maynard, Merrill, & Co.

> Some of Bryant's best poetic productions. Or eighth grade.

Sohrab and Rustum (Arnold). American Book Co.; Houghton, Mifflin, & Co.; Maynard & Merrill; Werner School Book Co.; Educational Publishing Co.

Style simple but highly poetic. Used also in eighth grade.

Cricket on the Hearth (Dickens). Houghton, Mifflin, & Co.; Maynard, Merrill, & Co.

Enoch Arden and the Lotus Eaters (Tennyson). Maynard, Merrill, & Co.; Houghton, Mifflin, & Co.; The Macmillan Co.; University Publishing Co.

Used in seventh and eighth grades and high schools.

Merchant of Venice (Shakespeare). American Book Co.; Ginn & Co.; The Macmillan Co.; D. C. Heath & Co.; Houghton, Mifflin, & Co.; Maynard & Merrill; Educational Publishing Co.; University Publishing Co.

The best of Shakespeare's for this grade. Parts of it are often dramatized and presented. Much liked by the children.

Tales of a Grandfather (Scott). Ginn & Co.; Educational Publishing Co.; University Publishing Co.

Stories of Wallace, Bruce, Douglas, and other Scotch heroes. Should be read only in parts in class. Library book.

Poems of Emerson. Houghton, Mifflin, & Co.

Historical and nature poems, with a good introduction. A small but important collection of poems for older children.

The Cotter's Saturday Night (Burns). Houghton, Mifflin, & Co.; Maynard, Merrill, & Co.

Contains also Tam O'Shanter and other poems of Burns's best.

Bunker Hill, Adams, and Jefferson (Webster). Houghton, Mifflin, & Co.; American Book Co.; Maynard, Merrill, & Co.

Historical, patriotic, and simple in style. The best of Webster's speeches for seventh and eighth grades.

Poor Richard's Almanac (Franklin). Houghton, Mifflin, & Co.

This contains also interesting papers and letters by Franklin. The proverbs of Franklin are well deserving the study of children.

Scudder's Life of Washington. Houghton, Mifflin, & Co.

Best life of Washington for grammar grades.

Source Book of American History (Hart). The Macmillan Co.

Excellent reading selections for sixth, seventh, and eighth grades.

Grandmother's Story and Other Poems (Holmes). Houghton, Mifflin, & Co.

Some of Holmes's best patriotic and humorous poems.

The Plant World (Vincent). D. Appleton & Co.

A superior collection of extracts from great scientific writers. One of the best science readers for upper grades.

Poetry of the Seasons (Lovejoy). Silver, Burdett, & Co.

    Good collection for reading and various uses.

William Tell (McMurry). Silver, Burdett, & Co.

    Suitable for seventh-grade reading. A drama.

Golden Treasury of Best Songs and Lyrical Poems (Palgrave). The Macmillan Co.

2. SUPPLEMENTARY AND REFERENCE BOOKS

Rules of Conduct (Washington). Houghton, Mifflin, & Co.

    Containing also his letters, farewell address, and other important papers.

Shakespeare's Tragedies (Lamb). American Book Co.; The Macmillan Co.

    Companion book to the Comedies.

Natural History of Selborne (White). Ginn & Co.

    A famous old book, interesting both in style and content. One of the first books of real nature study.

Letters (Chesterfield). Ginn & Co.; Maynard, Merrill, & Co. The Macmillan Co.

    Entertaining and unique. Valuable for reading extracts to the school.

Plutarch's Lives. Ginn & Co.; The Macmillan Co.; Educational Publishing Co.

    A book that all grammar school children should be encouraged to read.

The Two Great Retreats (Grote-Segur). Ginn & Co.

    Retreat of the ten thousand Greeks, and Napoleon's retreat from Russia.

The Alhambra (Irving). Ginn & Co.; Maynard, Merrill, & Co. The Macmillan Co.

    Most attractive descriptions and legends connected with the Alhambra.

Peter Schlemihl (Chamisso). Ginn & Co.

Picciola (Saintine). Ginn & Co.

Hatim Tai (from the Persian). Ginn & Co.

Life of Nelson (Southey). Ginn & Co.; American Book Co.; The Macmillan Co.

Camps and Firesides of the Revolution (Hart). The Macmillan Co.

    Interesting source material.

The Crofton Boys (Martineau). D. C. Heath & Co.

Orations on Washington and Landing of the Pilgrims (Webster). American Book Co.

    A few children may be encouraged to read these great speeches, among the best in our history. Somewhat difficult.

Silas Marner (Eliot). The Macmillan Co.; Sibley & Ducker; American Book Co.; Ginn & Co.; D. C. Heath & Co.; Houghton, Mifflin, & Co.; Educational Publishing Co.

> A good introduction for children to George Eliot's writings. Used in eighth grade and high school.

Vicar of Wakefield (Goldsmith). Ginn & Co.; American Book Co.; D. C. Heath & Co.; Houghton, Mifflin, & Co.; The Macmillan Co.; Maynard, Merrill, & Co.; Univ. Pub. Co.

> One of the great books, permeated with Goldsmith's fine style and humor.

Two Years Before the Mast (Dana). Houghton, Mifflin, & Co.

> A book of real power for boys and girls.

A Bunch of Herbs (Burroughs). Houghton, Mifflin, & Co.

> Good nature study for pupils and teachers. Also for regular reading.

Samuel Adams (Morse). Houghton, Mifflin, & Co.

> One of the best of American biographies. One of the best descriptions of scenes in Boston just preceding the Revolution.

Tom Brown's School Days (Hughes). The Macmillan Co.; Houghton, Mifflin, & Co.; Ginn & Co.; Educational Publishing Co.

> A story for boys. Vigorous and true to life.

Last of the Mohicans (Cooper). The Macmillan Co.; Maynard, Merrill, & Co.; D. C. Heath & Co.; Houghton, Mifflin, & Co.; University Publishing Co.

A good book with which to introduce young people to Cooper's famous stories.

Franklin's Autobiography. Ginn & Co.; Houghton, Mifflin, & Co.; Maynard, Merrill, & Co.; American Book Co.; The Macmillan Co.; The Educational Publishing Co.

> A book that all young people should read. Valuable in many ways.

Uncle Tom's Cabin (Stowe). Houghton, Mifflin, & Co.

> A library book for home reading.

From Colony to Commonwealth (Moore). Ginn & Co.

> Simple account of the early events of the Revolution about Boston.

Stories from the Classic Literature of Many Nations (Palmer). The Macmillan Co.

The Gold Bug and Other Tales (Poe). Houghton, Mifflin, & Co.

American War Ballads and Lyrics (Eggleston). G. P. Putnam's Sons.

The Siege of Leyden (Motley). D. C. Heath & Co.

Twelve Naval Captains. Scribner's Sons.

> Short biographies of naval heroes.

Open Sesame, Volume III. Ginn & Co.

    A collection for various uses, prose and verse. Patriotism, sentiment, humor, and nature.

Birddom (Keyser). D. Lothrop & Co.

    Good for regular reading. Written in the fine style of a true lover of nature.

Town Geology (Kingsley). The Macmillan Co.

    An interesting book for those predisposed to science.

Children's Stories of American Literature (1860-1896) (Wright). Scribner's Sons.

    Short biographies of recent American writers.

Prince and Pauper (Clemens). Harper & Bros.

3. TEACHERS' BOOKS

Education and the Larger Life (Henderson). Houghton, Mifflin, & Co.

    A book of great value to teachers for thoughtful study.

Critical Period of American History (Fiske). Houghton, Mifflin, & Co.

    A very superior and interesting book of the period just after the Revolution.

The Beginnings of New England (Fiske). Houghton, Mifflin, & Co.

    Valuable for sixth and seventh grade teachers.

Birds in the Bush (Torrey). Houghton, Mifflin, & Co.

    Entertaining nature study by a master.

Nestlings in Forest and Marsh (Wheelock). A. C. McClurg.

    A suggestive book for teachers and older pupils.

Madam How and Lady Why (Kingsley). The Macmillan Co.

    Interesting style and content.

Brave Little Holland (Griffis). Houghton, Mifflin, & Co.

    A historical study of the Dutch in Holland and in this country.

Familiar Flowers of Field and Garden (Matthews). D. Appleton & Co.

    An easy study of common plants and flowers according to the seasons.

Guy Mannering (Scott). Ginn & Co.

Autocrat of the Breakfast Table (Holmes). Houghton, Mifflin, & Co.

Tale of Two Cities (Dickens). Ginn & Co.; American Book Co.

Life of Pestalozzi (de Guimps). D. Appleton & Co.

First Bunker Hill Oration (Webster). D. C Heath & Co.

Mill on the Floss (George Eliot).

Hugh Wynne, Free Quaker (Mitchell). Century Co.

The Fortune of the Republic (Emerson). Houghton, Mifflin, & Co.

>Very stimulating to teachers.

Masterpieces of American Literature (Scudder). Houghton, Mifflin, & Co.

>One of the best collections of classical masterpieces.

Life of Samuel Johnson (Macaulay). Maynard, Merrill, & Co.; Houghton, Mifflin, & Co.

>Very fine, in Macaulay's superior style.

Modern Painters (Ruskin). Various publishers.

>For teachers, a good study in Ruskin.

Essay on Burns (Carlyle). Maynard, Merrill, & Co.; The Macmillan Co.; Houghton, Mifflin, & Co.; D. C. Heath & Co.; Educational Publishing Co.

>An interesting subject and an able treatment.

Readings from the Spectator. Educational Publishing Co.; Maynard, Merrill, & Co.

>Roger de Coverley and other selected parts of essays from Addison.

Six Centuries of English Poetry (Baldwin). Silver, Burdett, & Co.

>Valuable for reference and occasional study.

Fiske's Washington and His Country (Irving). Ginn & Co.

>Good life of Washington and history of the Revolution.

The War of Independence (Fiske). Houghton, Mifflin, & Co.

Poetic Interpretation of Nature (Shairp). Houghton, Mifflin, & Co.

Mere Literature (Woodrow Wilson). Houghton, Mifflin, & Co.

>An interesting series of essays for teachers.

The Life of Alexander Hamilton (Lodge). Houghton, Mifflin, & Co.

The Study and Teaching of English (Chubb). The Macmillan Co.

Burke's Speech on Conciliation with America. D. C. Heath & Co.; American Book Co.; The Macmillan Co.

EIGHTH GRADE

1. BOOKS FOR REGULAR READING LESSONS

Vision of Sir Launfal (Lowell). Houghton, Mifflin, & Co.; The Macmillan Co.

>One of the best poems in English for school use.

Julius Cæsar (Shakespeare). American Book Co.; The Macmillan Co.; Silver, Burdett, & Co.; D. C. Heath & Co.; Houghton, Mifflin, & Co.; Maynard, Merrill, & Co.; The Educational Publishing Co.; University Publishing Co.

>Well suited for eighth grade study and presentation. Used also in high schools.

Tales of a Wayside Inn (Longfellow). Houghton, Mifflin, & Co.

Bunker Hill, Adams, and Jefferson (Webster). Houghton, Mifflin, & Co.

Roger de Coverley (Addison). The Macmillan Co.; American Book Co.; Houghton, Mifflin, & Co.; The Educational Publishing Co.; Silver, Burdett, & Co.; Sibley & Ducker; D. C. Heath & Co.; Maynard, Merrill, & Co.

>An excellent study for children in eighth grade. Also used in high schools.

In Bird Land (Keyser). A. C. McClurg & Co.

>A book adapted to awaken the children to a sympathetic observation of birds.

Lady of the Lake (Scott). Maynard, Merrill, & Co.; American Book Co.; Ginn & Co.; Houghton, Mifflin, & Co.; The Macmillan Co.; D. C. Heath & Co.; The Educational Publishing Co.; University Publishing Co.

>An attractive study. Somewhat difficult.

Marmion (Scott). Ginn & Co.; Maynard, Merrill, & Co.; The Macmillan Co.; The Educational Publishing Co.; Houghton, Mifflin, & Co.; American Book Co.

>A great historical picture, full of interest.

The Great Debate (Hayne-Webster). Houghton, Mifflin, & Co.; Maynard, Merrill, & Co.

>A fine study of forensic debate. Incidentally a deeper appreciation of history. Somewhat difficult for eighth grade.

A Bunch of Herbs (Burroughs). Houghton, Mifflin, & Co.

>A very suggestive study of common plants, trees, weather, etc.

Burke on Conciliation. Sibley & Ducker; Ginn & Co.; The Macmillan Co.; Silver, Burdett, & Co.; Houghton, Mifflin, & Co.; American Book Co.; D. C. Heath & Co.; Maynard, Merrill, & Co. Used also in high school.

>A great study both as literature and as history. One of the best studies in American history before the Revolution.

The Gettysburg Speech (Lincoln). Houghton, Mifflin, & Co.

>The inaugurals, an essay by Lowell on Lincoln and other papers.

The Deserted Village, and The Traveller (Goldsmith). The Macmillan Co.; Houghton, Mifflin, & Co.; Maynard, Merrill, & Co.

The best of Goldsmith's poems. Also shorter poems.

Franklin's Autobiography. The Macmillan Co.; Ginn & Co.; Houghton, Mifflin, & Co.; Maynard, Merrill, & Co.; American Book Co.; The Educational Publishing Co.

Partly for class use and partly for reference reading.

Plutarch's Lives. Ginn & Co.; The Educational Publishing Co.; The Macmillan Co.

A few for class reading. Others for reference.

Translation of Homer's Odyssey (Palmer). Houghton, Mifflin, & Co.

Abraham Lincoln (Schurz). Houghton, Mifflin, & Co.

Two Great Retreats (Grote-Segur). Ginn & Co.

Good sight reading, and for reference.

Peter the Great (Motley). Maynard, Merrill, & Co.

A very interesting essay in superior style.

The Succession of Forest Trees, Wild Apples, and Sounds (Thoreau). Houghton, Mifflin, & Co.

A very attractive nature study.

2. SUPPLEMENTARY AND REFERENCE BOOKS

Ruskin's Selections. Ginn & Co.; The Macmillan Co.

Longer selections from Ruskin. Excellent also for regular reading.

My Hunt after the Captain, etc. (Holmes). Houghton, Mifflin, & Co.

A very entertaining description of scenes during war times.

Don Quixote (Cervantes). Ginn & Co.; The Macmillan Co.; Scribner's Sons.

A book that children should be encouraged to read. Its satire and humor they should learn to appreciate.

Ivanhoe (Scott). The Macmillan Co.; Ginn & Co.; American Book Co.; Houghton, Mifflin, & Co.; D. C. Heath & Co.

The best introduction to Scott's novels, in connection with school studies.

The Abbot (Scott). Ginn & Co.; American Book Co.

One of Scott's best stories.

Yesterdays with Authors (James T. Fields). Houghton, Mifflin, & Co.

Rob Roy, and Quentin Durward (Scott). Ginn & Co.; American Book Co.

Good library books.

The House of Seven Gables (Hawthorne). Houghton, Mifflin, & Co.

    A New England story in Hawthorne's style. A good home study for children and teachers.

The Boy's Browning. Dana, Estes, & Co.

    A good collection of the simpler poems adapted to younger readers.

Tale of Two Cities (Dickens). Ginn & Co.; American Book Co.

Jean Valjean (from Les Miserables). Ginn & Co.; Educational Publishing Co.

The Talisman (Scott). American Book Co.; Ginn & Co.

Treasure Island (Stevenson). Scribner's Sons.

Life of Washington (Statesmen Series). Houghton, Mifflin, & Co.

Life of Nelson (Southey). The Macmillan Co.; Ginn & Co.; American Book Co.

The Foot-path Way (Torrey). Houghton, Mifflin, & Co.

    One of the best books for cultivating an appreciation for nature.

In Bird Land (Keyser). A. C. McClurg & Co.

    A very interesting bird study.

The Old Manse, and A Few Mosses (Hawthorne). Houghton, Mifflin, & Co.

    A pleasing account of the old house and its associations.

News from the Birds (Keyser). D. Appleton & Co.

    Excellent study and observation.

Peasant and Prince (Martineau). Ginn & Co.; Univ. Pub. Co.

    An interesting narrative of French life just before the Revolution.

A Book of Famous Verse (Repplier). Houghton, Mifflin, & Co.

    A superior collection of poems.

Nature Pictures by American Poets (Marble). The Macmillan Co.

    Choice poems descriptive of nature.

Seven British Classics. American Book Co.

    A good collection of English masterpieces. Adapted also for regular reading in seventh and eighth grades.

Star Land (Ball). Ginn & Co.

    A very interesting and well-written introduction to astronomy.

Life of John Quincy Adams (Morse). Houghton, Mifflin, & Co.

    The Statesmen Series.

Poems of American Patriotism (Matthews). Scribner's Sons.

3. TEACHERS' BOOKS

Culture and Anarchy (Arnold). Maynard, Merrill, & Co.

    It illustrates well Arnold's thought and style.

Elaine (Tennyson). Maynard, Merrill, & Co.; The Macmillan Co.

    A beautiful poem, simple and musical, from the Idylls of the King.

Great Words of Great Americans (Putnam).

    Papers and addresses of Washington and Lincoln.

Literature in Schools (Scudder). Houghton, Mifflin, & Co.

    A stimulating book for teachers of all grades.

The Princess (Tennyson). Ginn & Co.; The Macmillan Co.; Maynard, Merrill, & Co.; American Book Co.

Biblical Masterpieces (Moulton). The Macmillan Co.

The Book Lover (Baldwin). A. C. McClurg & Co.

    A discussion of books and reading with lists of books and suggestions.

The Story of the Birds (Baskett). D. Appleton & Co.

    One of the superior books of nature study.

Frail Children of the Air (Scudder). Houghton, Mifflin, & Co.

    A scientific but simple treatise on butterflies.

Books and Culture (Mabie). Dodd, Mead, & Co.

    An attractive and valuable book on literature for teachers.

Science Sketches (Jordan). A. C. McClurg & Co.

    A very attractive style in the treatment of scientific topics.

Birds through an Opera Glass (Merriam). Houghton, Mifflin, & Co.

    Good outdoor study.

Up and Down the Brooks (Bramford). Houghton, Mifflin, & Co.

    A study of insect life in the streams.

Essays, first series (Emerson). Houghton, Mifflin, & Co.

    Essays on history, self-reliance, compensation, and others. Teachers should study Emerson's essays.

Heroes and Hero-Worship (Carlyle). A. C. McClurg & Co.; The Macmillan Co.

    A great book and a good specimen of Carlyle's style and thought.

Introductory Lessons in English (McNeil and Lynch). American Book Co.

> A series of masterpieces with questions and discussions as to treatment in high schools.

How to Teach Reading (Clark). Scott, Forsman, & Co.

> A pedagogical treatment of reading.

Counsel upon the Reading of Books (Van Dyke). Houghton, Mifflin, & Co.

> Strong essays on books and reading from different points of view by strong writers.

Romola (George Eliot). Various publishers.

> One of the great novels. Valuable in many ways.

Macbeth (Shakespeare). Silver, Burdett, & Co.; D. C. Heath & Co.; The Macmillan Co.; American Book Co.; The Educational Publishing Co.; University Publishing Co.

> This and other great plays of Shakespeare should be read by teachers.

Life of Hamilton (Statesmen Series). Houghton, Mifflin, & Co.

Emerson's Self-Reliance. Maynard, Merrill, & Co.

Life of Webster (Lodge), also John Quincy Adams (Morse). Houghton, Mifflin, & Co.

    From the Statesmen Series. Excellent reading for the teacher.

Literary Study of the Bible (Moulton). D. C. Heath & Co.

    A valuable introduction to the literary appreciation of the Bible.

The Marble Faun (Hawthorne). Houghton, Mifflin, & Co.

Plutarch's Lives. Ginn & Co.; The Macmillan Co.; The Educational Publishing Co.

Locke's Thoughts on Education. The Macmillan Co.

Spencer's Education. D. Appleton & Co.

Daniel Deronda (George Eliot).

Dombey and Son (Charles Dickens).

The Autobiography of John Stuart Mill.

The Schoolmaster in Comedy and Satire (Skinner). The American Book Co.

Emerson's American Scholar. American Book Co.; Houghton, Mifflin, & Co.; Maynard, Merrill, & Co.

The Judgment of Socrates. Houghton, Mifflin, & Co.

Poets and Problems (Cooke). Houghton, Mifflin, & Co.

Introduction to Tennyson, Ruskin, and Browning.

A Century of Science and other Essays (Fiske). Houghton, Mifflin, & Co.

American Writers of To-day (Vedder). Silver, Burdett, & Co.

Ralph Waldo Emerson (Holmes). American Men of Letters Series. Houghton, Mifflin, & Co.